BUILDING YOUR INCLUSIVE CLASSROOM

Building Your Inclusive Classroom explores why we need to adapt our teaching – and our approaches to children and young people – and how this will support the achievement of everyone in the classroom, including the teacher. It will help educators in mainstream settings, across all key stages, to adapt not only their resources but also their approaches for children with Special Educational Needs and/or Disabilities (SEND) and their peers.

This accessible resource provides a toolkit of ideas, methods, and motivation to enable teachers to make their classrooms fully inclusive. Chapters present the most effective evidence-based approaches – exploring both relational, restorative practice and traditional methods – to provide the foundations upon which to build inclusive classrooms. The book:

- Offers practical suggestions along with examples and case studies
- Includes reflective questions to encourage readers to consider their current settings
- Provides clear summaries and breakdowns of key guidelines and concepts
- Does the heavy lifting for you and presents evidence-based approaches in an engaging manner
- Incorporates the voices of staff and parents throughout
- Inspires the reader to take risks, enhance current practice, and to make meaningful change for children and young people.

Adaptive teaching has traversed beyond just the mini-whiteboard and the writing frame, and we need now, more than ever, to differentiate and adapt our approaches too, for children both with and without diagnosed SEND. This book will be essential reading for mainstream teachers, Special Educational Needs and/or Disabilities Co-ordinators (SENDCOs), and trainee teachers, across all key stages.

Verity Lush is a SENDCO within a mainstream all-through school (ages 4–16). She has been teaching for 20 years but it was upon joining a specialist SEND provision in 2014 that she became a passionate advocate for children with SEND. Verity's current school is set within a diverse, inner-city area, in a school that now feels like family to her. She firmly believes that relationships are at the core of everything.

BUILDING YOUR INCLUSIVE CLASSROOM

A Toolkit for Adaptive Teaching and Relational Practice

Verity Lush

Routledge
Taylor & Francis Group

LONDON AND NEW YORK

Designed cover image: © Getty Images

First published 2024
by Routledge
4 Park Square, Milton Park, Abingdon, Oxon OX14 4RN

and by Routledge
605 Third Avenue, New York, NY 10158

Routledge is an imprint of the Taylor & Francis Group, an informa business

© 2024 Verity Lush

British Library Cataloguing-in-Publication Data
A catalogue record for this book is available from the British Library

ISBN: 978-1-032-55991-9 (hbk)
ISBN: 978-1-032-55989-6 (pbk)
ISBN: 978-1-003-43326-2 (ebk)

DOI: 10.4324/b23417

Typeset in Interstate
by Deanta Global Publishing Services, Chennai, India

For Ashley, India and Amelie.

CONTENTS

ACKNOWLEDGEMENTS

This book has been bobbing about in my head, in one shape or another, for the past decade, and I am so grateful to everybody who has contributed to my transferring it onto the written page. Thank you also to anyone who has taken the time – and who has cared enough about the young people we work with – to read it.

With 'thank you' in mind, I'd like to say a big one to everybody at Routledge Publishing, who has supported me in this endeavour. To Clare Ashworth, who saw the potential of this book from the off and without whom it wouldn't exist as it does. You helped me to see the woods as opposed to just the wordy trees – thank you. Some of your feedback moved me to tears (for the avoidance of doubt, the happy variety!). True emotional literacy in action.

Thank you also to Molly Kavanagh, whose support – particularly when seeking permissions – was utterly invaluable. You have no idea how much I appreciated this. Thanks also go to Stephanie Derbyshire, Hannah Champney and Ellen Murray for their support with this project.

Before I move onto other thanks, I am also grateful to the Education Endowment Foundation for allowing me permission to use their work in this book – and I'd like to extend that thanks to all other publishers and authors who kindly did so. In particular, Dan Hughes, Charles Feltman, Martin Wood of Worth Publishing, Mark Finnis, and Sue Phillips.

When I first started teaching, I didn't expect to one day specialise in the area of SEND; however, thanks to a wonderful school that does, it transpired to be my path. Those of you who are reading this and who have worked at that particular school will know exactly what I mean. Thank you all, past and present.

Writing a book on the side whilst having an all-consuming day job is no easy feat, so I am incredibly thankful to the people and the team around me during said day job. Their infinite support, propensity for fun, and sheer resilience are a thing to behold. In no particular order, there are plenty whom I would like to thank. Your hard work, passion, and downright in-it-for-the-kids attitude is what it's all about.

Laine Fletcher (the glue that holds our wonderful department together, there aren't enough thanks in the world), Jasmine Dale (a relational and inclusive champion if ever there was one; believe in yourself), Claire Swinson (as kind as kind gets, sparkle personified, with pink nails to boot), Jacky Evans (fabulous hair and many a daily cackle, for which I thank you!), Steve Flores (master of the death-stare and a fantastic HoH), Erika Anders (as ever, whether it's juggling life or juicing, I don't know how you do it), Jo Webb (all the excel skills and my right-hand woman, thank you), Carly Reid (a true ironwoman and a phenomenal inspiration), Alex Franklin (who always manages to look excited as opposed to weeping when she sees me coming towards her), Hayley Taylor ('turn around' – the Year 11 Leavers' vid is fresh in my mind as I write this), lovely Rachael Colmer and wonderful Hannah Hughes (I've obviously had to co-join you guys as part of our little triad!), Fiona Rogers (cats – I mean, what more *is there*?!), Mel Trise (one day Ant and Dec will take you to Florida), Yve Butterworth (who will gamely turn her hand to anything that's asked of her), Anna Doyle (an all-round star), Claire Stonebridge (a fab Learning Support Assistant for our young people), and last but absolutely not least, Sharon Shaw, the smoothest Access Arrangement tester in the South (until she moved back up North – number 9!).

Thanks also to our *entire* school family. I don't have the word count to thank you all, but this is a heartfelt shout-out: Team Mayfield, past, present, future. That team may change over the years, but the determination to get the best for the young people in our care never does. A few names, but by no means exhaustive: Phil and Becky Denford, Steve Reid, James Campbell, Emma Radford-Groom, Kirsty Rolfe, Alison Barnicott, Alison Rowland, Karin Gardner, Joe Houghton-Gisby, Varsha Durve, Amanda Foster, David Sharkey, David Wheat, Sharon Rolfe (quiz night Queen!), Michele John, George Rolfe (who always asks how I am – and actually listens to the reply), Caroline Nicholls, Julie Winzar, Lynne Hollis, Andy Tite, Alix Beech, Michael Godfrey (my Google Form skills are shocking, thank goodness yours are stellar!), Rich Clark-Lyons, Jude Firth, and Jen Lewis. You all make my days merrier and the lives of our children brighter: thank you.

To Claire Mason, Jane Steggall, and Feleena Elkington – I have learnt so much from you, thank you. Our links with you guys as external agencies are simply invaluable.

To my buddy of so many, many years, Anneke Ring, thank you. And to Liz Davies, whether it's Fridays like it used to be, or Wednesdays like it is now, it's sacrosanct! Thank you.

Thanks also to Jodi Webb – our 'new leaf' in Spanish was a joke turning-point that turned into a true turning-point for me.

Cath Drinkwater, you may have flown away to the Land Down Under, but you're with me in spirit every day – thank goodness we don't have to pay the 1992 landline bill to stay in touch now.

To Mrs Sheila Ridley (I would not be where I am and who I am without you), and to Steve Gerlach, whom I have lost touch with across the years but whom I still think of regularly – how I loved our department.

For the Front Table – you know! Charlotte Baker, Lynne Lister and Becky Maddox.

To Watson and Moriarty, you're cats and you can't read (and I'm not sure whether it's me you love or the food I provide, though I can guess), but you kept me company by curling up next to me whilst I wrote this book.

And to my wonderful, funny, mischievous mum, Janet McGill – I absolutely love you, thank you for all that you are, and all that you encourage me to be. With love and thanks also to Peter – who is, of course, Dolly the Dog's favourite.

To India and Amelie. Gorgeous girls. I love you. You've championed this book from the start, even though it meant my hibernating at a laptop for many a Sunday. You are both an absolute wonder to me; I have no idea how I got so lucky. Grab your dreams poppets and make them realities. I want you to have it all.

And finally, for Ashley. Absolutely for Ashley. There aren't many husbands who'd recognise this book as being a love letter from their wives, so it's a good job I'm yours. Education has been the thread running through our lives for the past two decades, and it's from you that I've learnt the most. You always have been, and will remain to be, the most inspirational human being I have ever met – you are solely in it for the kids. It's all about relationships, and I am so thankful for ours; it's as you said it would be. And I love you.

Introduction
We Can Be Heroes

Teaching. It's an idealistic profession. We go into it to change the world. We watch education secretaries come, we watch education secretaries go. We get accused by pockets of the tabloid press of being lazy, of hiding during worldwide pandemics and closing schools, of taking too many holidays, and yet - *and yet* - folk still enter this profession. And the vast majority of the people with whom I initially trained to teach, 20 years ago, are still teaching today.

Why is this, when teaching can be so incredibly tough? Presumably because, as many of us reading this will know, it's also *incredibly satisfying*. We strive for the ideal. None of us went into teaching, bright-eyed and bushy-tailed, yearning to get kicked in the shins by a 6-year-old and being informed as to which orifice we should insert our whiteboard markers. We went into it to make the clichéd 'difference', but, as with so many clichés, it's true. We do make a difference - a positive, impactful, meaningful difference. And anybody who believes that teachers clock off at 3pm, or that we are a lazy breed of ingrates, should come and do a day in the classroom.

Teaching is a ride. It's a vertigo-inducing blast of a journey, and we are on it with young people and children who may not yet know how to control their own emotions, let alone respond appropriately to anyone else's. We are entertainers, we are planners, we are negotiators, and we are in loco parentis. We are hard, hard workers and each day is a new beginning. Each lesson is a new start. We pick ourselves up and we go again, we persist, and we rise to the challenge. We effect positive change in the lives of young people each and every day - even when they do not acknowledge or realise it, and when we sometimes do not realise it ourselves.

This book rests on the premise that, as part of your role as a teacher, you wish to ensure that you are **inclusive**, and that every child in your classroom is catered for. This is no mean feat, but the fact that you are reading this already suggests that your classroom and your ethos is one of inclusivity, where children feel valued, and where you want to strive for the best. In a post-pandemic world, teaching has become more challenging - yet therefore more rewarding - than ever before.

The past decade has impacted significantly on our young people, whether they have Special Educational Needs and/or Disabilities (SEND) or not. Screentime plus social media multiplied by a pandemic, does not a functioning society make. Hopefully, this book will provoke thought and discussion, enabling and empowering you to make changes to not only your lessons and your delivery, but to your approaches for children with SEND - and, more than that, it will benefit your teaching for all students, 'Good teaching for pupils with SEND is good teaching for all' (Education Endowment Foundation 2020). In fact, I think we can set our aspirations even higher, and aim for excellence. We won't always hit the heady heights of that benchmark, but we can benefit our young people all the more if we try.

DOI: 10.4324/b23417-1

Whilst this book is not a magic wand, it will, I hope, support you to think, encourage you to reflect, perhaps empower you to take some risks with your teaching and to employ your creativity, ultimately inspiring you to try new approaches. It will also provide practical ideas and strategies, beyond the more traditional aspects of, as the Early Career Framework (Department for Education 2019) states, 'adaptive teaching'. This differs from the 'differentiation' of yesteryear, and is more responsive, more inclusive, and rests very much on our knowing the children in front of us.

Adaptation itself is something that we all do, all of the time. We adapt our manner when the head teacher pops into our classroom. If a member of the Senior Leadership Team (SLT) nips in, we straighten up. If our mate comes in, our shoulders drop and we might engage in the well-practised Teacher Sigh and possibly an eye roll – with the depth of the former dependent on the kind of day we are having. We adapt how we speak to our mothers compared to how we speak to our best friends.

Adaptation is natural, it is not something to be scared of, yet when we get an email from the Learning Support Department or the Special Educational Needs and Disabilities Co-ordinator (SENDCO) telling us that we need to do 'this for child X' and 'that for child Y', we may have a tendency to think to ourselves, 'and just how on earth do you think I can do that as well as planning for a class of 29 other individuals?!'

However, adaptive teaching doesn't mean you have to make (or should make) a time-consuming different resource to scaffold work for each student with additional needs – adaptations take many forms to support inclusion and go far beyond the writing frame, traversing instead into the realms of our relationships and our approaches. And that's what makes this book a little different, because it proposes that not only should we adapt our **teaching**, but – due to what 'teaching' is in a 21st-century society – we need to adapt our **approaches** to young people, too. We need to build a solid foundation of **relational practice** in our classrooms, and progress with all else from that starting point.

This book has essentially done the heavy-lifting for you when it comes to relational approaches. In it, you'll find the **what**, the **why**, and the **how** of evidence-based relational approaches, with 4 key pedagogies to draw from, and practical strategies to use and employ in your classroom and school. Everything in life begins with relationships and the classroom is no different. Until we get these right, nothing else can follow. We have to reach the children before we can truly teach the children, and this book will support you in doing both.

In essence, this book is a toolkit for building your inclusive classroom from the ground up. The toolkit is going to support you in constructing your inclusive home – your classroom – and the key to the door is **consistency**. The foundation of your home, the solid block on which it stands that must remain stable, will be your **relational approach**. The bricks with which you build – and that may need repointing from time to time – will be your curriculum and planning. At times you will need to employ scaffolding in your classroom, but scaffolding is only ever a temporary measure for any home. It comes and goes and it's all about knowing when we need it, and when we don't.

Finally, I'd like to turn to the words of William Blake (if we excuse his less-than-inclusive terminology). Blake said, that 'if the doors of perception were cleansed everything would appear to man as it is: Infinite' (1975). Children's perceptive abilities – whether they have no

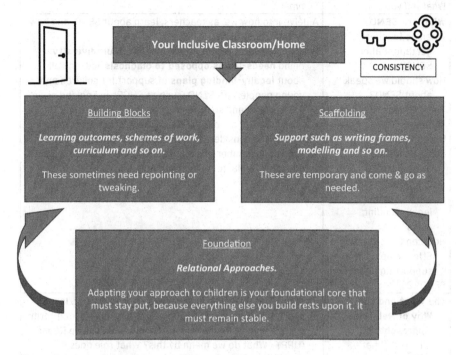

Figure 0.1 A model for your inclusive classroom

additional need or significant SEND – are endless. As teachers, we are in the truly privileged position of facilitating the opening of those doors, and the key to those doors is consistency. Consistency of strict boundaries, of unconditional positive regard, and of championing needs-led inclusion.

Being a hero is not just the stuff of which movies are made. If you're in teaching, you already are one. Every day.

What You'll Find in Each Chapter

Chapter	What will you find?	Summary
1	**Meeting Needs** Who am I? Relationships Looking after yourself and wellbeing The meaning of 'inclusion' Adaptive teaching or differentiation?	An introduction to me – given that this book is all about **relationships** and the importance of getting to know one another! We'll look at **what** and **who** led us into teaching, how to look after **ourselves** before we can look after others, what **inclusion** means, and the differences between 'differentiation' and 'adaptive teaching'.

Chapter	What will you find?	Summary
2	**What are SEND?** When do teachers get taught about SEND? How should we speak about SEND? The 4 Broads Areas of Need Neurodiversity Being needs-led as opposed to diagnosis-led Support plan and legally-binding plans How can Cause and Effect help us in supporting needs? SENDCOs	A delve into how we, as teachers, learn about SEND, and how to **talk** about SEND. We'll look at the 4 Broad Areas of SEND, **neurodiversity**, being **needs-led as opposed to diagnosis-led**, and all about **legally-binding plans** of support for children and young people with SEND (such as EHCPs in England or an IDP in Wales and so on). We'll also look at a model of **Cause and Effect** for supporting needs, and consider what the **SENDCO** does in schools – the only member of school staff who is required to be educated to Masters Level and hold QTS.
3	**The What and the Why of Relational Approaches** Part 1 – The 'What' of Relational Approaches Part 2 – The 'Why' of Relational Approaches	**Part 1** – What relational approaches are and are not. In short, they're not a soft touch, and they lead to long-term success and last a lifetime. Unconditional Positive Regard (UPR) – What do we mean by this? What role does it play in relational approaches? **Part 2** – Why we need to embed relational approaches, looking at **Maslow's Hierarchy of Needs**, SEMH, relationships outside of school, screentime and devices, **Adverse Childhood Experiences (ACEs)**, being readily available trusted adults, trauma recovery and attachment disorders.
4	**The 'How' of Relational Approaches** **Four Core Approaches with Which to Build Your Foundation** Part 1 – Emotional Literacy Part 2 – Nurture Part 3 – Restorative/ Relational Practice Part 4 – PACE (Playfulness, Acceptance, Curiosity and Empathy)	**Part 1** – How to use our **emotional intelligence** in our classrooms and around our schools. **Part 2** – The **6 Principles of Nurture** and how to embed them in our classrooms, underpinned by emotional intelligence. **Part 3** – How restorative practice can change **culture and ethos**, underpinned by emotional intelligence. **Part 4** – How employing a **PACE approach** allows young people to feel safe in our classrooms, and to flourish, underpinned by emotional intelligence.

Chapter	What will you find?	Summary
5	**Evidence-Based Adaptive Teaching and How to Do It** Part 1 - Evidence-Based Recommendations for Adaptive Teaching Part 2 - Practical Ideas for Adaptive Teaching Part 3 - Using Playfulness (PACE) to Adapt Planning and Resources	**Part 1** - 2 evidence-based approaches for **high quality teaching.** Firstly, we'll touch on **Rosenshine's 10 Principles of Instruction** (2012), which give excellent and concise guidance. Secondly, we'll consider high quality teaching specifically for children with additional needs, by examining the more recent work of the **Education Endowment Foundation** (EEF) and their Guidance Report for SEND in mainstream schools (2020). **Part 2** - Part 2 will give you practical ideas, based around the **5 strategies** advised by the EEF: 1) Flexible grouping 2) Cognitive and metacognitive strategies 3) Explicit instruction 4) Using technology to support pupils with SEND 5) Scaffolding. **Part 3** - How to use our understanding of **relational practice** (specifically **PACE**) to adapt our resources and planning for the children and young people in our inclusive classroom. We'll consider both **why** we need to do this, and **how** to do this. This will include practical, engaging ideas and encouragement to be *creative*! It will also include a look at **experiential learning and stories** which can be an excellent addition to our teaching toolkit for all children and especially those with SEMH needs.
6	**A Need-to-Know Basis Pulling It All Together** Documents of support - how would you now use them, incorporating all of our learning from Chapters 1-5? How are you going to juggle all this?! Getting into the habit of adaptive teaching	This will include an exemplar of 2 **documents detailing needs** that our Learning Support Departments might give us, in this case a '**Pupil Passport**' (known by various names). We need to remember our model of **Cause and Effect**, with a recap of the **Toolkit** for building our inclusive classroom. Given everything that we have covered in our previous chapters, how would you use the documents? How can you recognise what to use and where? And why it's easier than we think to teach in an adaptive and responsive manner - particularly as opposed to traditional 'differentiation'. **We can do this!**
7	**What About the Adults?** **Parents, Carers and Support Staff**	Inclusion means all of us. How to make the best out of the adults in your classroom - we'll look at some guidance around this - and how to build those relationships with parents and carers.
	A Final Word	One last, hopefully motivational, word before you go forth and build your inclusive classroom!
	Appendix	An at-a-glance table guide to **how** and **where** each chapter of this book links to the 5 Recommendations of the EEF's Guidance Report for SEND in Mainstream Schools.

References

Blake, W. (1975). *The Marriage of Heaven and Hell*. Oxford: OUP.

Department for Education. (2019). *Early Career Framework*. Available at: https://assets.publishing. service.gov.uk/government/uploads/system/uploads/attachment_data/file/978358/Early-Career_ Framework_April_2021.pdf

Education Endowment Foundation. (2020, updated 2021). *SEND in Mainstream Schools. A Guidance Report*. Available at: https://educationendowmentfoundation.org.uk/education-evidence/guidance-reports/send

Rosenshine, B. (2012). Principles of Instruction: Research-Based Strategies That All Teachers Should Know. *American Educator*, 36(1), pp. 12–39. Available at: https://www.aft.org/sites/default/files/ Rosenshine.pdf

Chapter One

Meeting Needs (Including Your Own)

Chapter 1	A Summary
Meeting Needs	An introduction to me – given that this book is all about **relationships** and the importance of getting to know one another! We'll look at **what** and **who** led us into teaching, how to look after **ourselves** before we can look after others, what **inclusion** means, and the differences between 'differentiation' and 'adaptive teaching'.

Who Am I To Be Telling You How to Teach?

(Spoiler: I Will Not Be Doing That!)

This book is about inspiration. It's about inspiring one another to be the best that we can be, and it's about inspiring the exact same in our students: each and every one of them. To teach, and to be successful in doing so, requires a positive mindset. We are continually striving for progress, for achievement, and for success. And again, this is for both ourselves and the children in our lessons.

Everyone in teaching has something to bring to the table. Ideas and suggestions, innovations, and ways in which to adapt approaches. Sometimes, due to the tough realities of the job, we can see ourselves or perhaps other colleagues becoming a little beleaguered by this as opposed to enthused, and the aim of this book is instead to ignite our enthusiasm! It is not about telling you how to teach; it's about sharing evidence-based advice and catching aflame those sparks of joy that we all experience when we know that we are the ones who have enabled a student to *get it*. We are the ones who have supported a child in both **being** and **feeling** successful.

This book is absolutely not about telling you what to do or about saying who knows best (indeed, does anyone know best?!). Instead, it's about questioning, about working together, and about examining different ideas and approaches to try. We've all experienced being patronised, quietly simmering and calling ourselves 'granny' whilst somebody else teaches us to 'suck eggs', and it's no different in school. As staff, we sit through training sessions and it's sometimes hard, especially at the end of a long day, to try and remain open-minded as regards what is being delivered. But however long we either have or have not been at it, there's always something new to learn or implement, or something to refresh

DOI: 10.4324/b23417-2

in teaching – something to be excited about or inspired by, and that's what this book is for. It's to develop ourselves and our practice, to take risks perhaps and try new things, and to consider our approaches to children whilst we do it.

This book is written under no assumption that I am an omniscient oracle of adaptive teaching. Instead, I am hoping that the amalgamation of training, research and experience that I have collated – over the past decade in particular – will save you the hassle of doing so. And I am also hoping that, when you read it, you might then be inspired to share your own ideas and experiences, because everyone in teaching is learning all the time; it's never just the children and young people who learn inside the classroom. Sometimes, we even need to *unlearn* things in order to progress.

Are there things that you've had to '**unlearn**' in your career? Do you think 'unlearning' is sometimes as important as learning?

What have you had to reflect on or change?

Have you had to support children in 'unlearning' as opposed to 'learning'? How easy is it (or how hard) to unlearn something that we've already **embedded**?

Relationships

A core concept that makes this book about adaptive teaching slightly different to others is the foundation of relational approaches that I am propounding as being key to all else, and the idea of then adapting our teaching using these. I have done some of the heavy lifting here for you regarding research into such approaches (see Chapters 3 and 4), but also – because I believe that everything starts with healthy, strong relationships – it seems to make sense if I share something about me and how I've come to the conclusion that, in my opinion, this philosophy is a central tenet of inclusion.

Very often, we go into teaching having been influenced by something or someone linked to our own past experiences of education. How many of us can say that it was a particular teacher, or lesson, or school experience that was the cause of our chosen career path, with teaching as the consequential effect? I suspect the answer is myriad. Not all of these experiences or people will have been positive. Sometimes it is the negatives that motivate us to go out into the world and ensure that we ourselves achieve the positives instead. Hopefully though, it's also the inspirational staff who taught us that made us think, 'I want to do this too!' or 'I want to be like them!' Once we become teachers, it can be hard to imagine that there will be children in our schools who look at us and decide that they'd quite like to be doing what we are doing. But what a privileged position we are therefore in! The crux of our ambition is to change the world, even just a smidge, and this then gains more momentum, like a domino effect, when we ourselves inspire others to also teach.

What's **your story** about how you got into teaching?

Who or what **inspired** you to teach?

If it was one of your own teachers, have you ever contacted them and told them?

In terms of my own ambitions, I had wanted to teach from a young age, but the direction that my career has taken – particularly towards inclusion – definitely stems from my own experiences of school. I went to a private girls' school but had a significantly different background to many of my friends. Most of their parents were professionals – solicitors, dentists, anaesthetists, and so on – whereas I was at the school by virtue of my mother's determination, and my grandfather and dad owning a second-hand car business, a pub, and a pool hall. Other kids lived in huge houses on the seafront, whereas I lived in a (perfectly lovely) terraced house at the deprived end of the city. However, as a child visiting huge properties with swimming pools, and even one with an observatory in the roof, I could see the difference. I didn't think much of it; I was an only child with a strong sense of self embedded in me by my family. However, there were comments that friends sometimes inadvertently let slip that had originated from their parents, and it's usually the little things like this that make us feel different as kids, even when we are too young to understand why. As children, we often experience our first feelings of exclusion at the hands of other children.

My parents had divorced when I was 8 years old, unusual in those days and another marker of being slightly different to the pack, and my father was an alcoholic. I adored my dad. He was a loving, charismatic man, but the embarrassment of his arriving to the nativity play late and sitting at the opposite end of a bench to my mother – with only blank space in between them – was not lost on me. Stuff like this is crippling when you're a kid, and the fact that I still recall it now makes me think about the children and young people in school today and the effect that such instances in their own lives have on them.

When I was 12 years old, my father died, very suddenly, of a massive asthma attack. It was on an April Wednesday and when I sat on my bed to complete my maths homework, I had no idea that my little world was about to topple on its axis. A knock on the door and the entirely unexpected arrival of my grandfather – bearing news that must have been incomprehensible for him to deliver – changed everything, and, as all of us who have lost someone will recognise, it has impacted everything in my life from that point on, whether in small, drip-fed ways, or vast oceans of difference. And, as an adult, and especially once I started teaching, the thing that really stood out for me in the days following his passing was that *not one* teacher at my school mentioned it to me. I returned to school 48 hours later, on the Friday of that week, and when a classmate asked me why I had not been in school the previous day, it was the first time that I had to experience the horror of telling somebody that my dad had died. My dad had done what was, at that tender age, unfathomable. I cried when I managed to voice the words, and my tutor took me outside into the hallway. She straightened my shirt, did up my top button for me, patted my shoulders, and sent me back into the classroom, but not once did she mention her knowledge that, since she had last seen me on the Wednesday afternoon, my father had suddenly passed away. Not once did she enquire as to whether I was ok, or tell me who I could speak to, or ask if I'd like to ring my mum. And I don't say this with any blame or bitterness – this was 1989 and conversations like those just weren't had – and so I say it simply as fact, and as fact that demonstrates a core difference between teaching then and teaching now. There was no Emotional Literacy Support Assistant (ELSA) in 1989, there was no Mental Health Support Team (MHST); there wasn't even mention of 'mental health' as a concept. There wasn't even mention of the death of a parent.

Fast-forward to the 21st century and it is, thankfully, unheard of that a child would return to school after such a life-changing experience without having immediate support in place. From the very start of my career, my own experiences as a child deeply influenced my approach to teaching. No doubt yours have done the same for you. I probably have a natural leaning toward emotional intelligence and what makes people tick, because I subsequently followed a path that was initially subject-based, as a lead for Religious Studies, Philosophy and Ethics, and I had been especially inspired by my own RS teacher, a Mrs Sheila Ridley. Mrs Ridley spoke to students like they were humans, with voices that were worth listening to and with opinions that were worth hearing – in essence, she was inclusive, and I wanted to be like her. It was after the birth of my youngest daughter that I happened to then fall into the specialist path of inclusion and Special Educational Needs and/or Disabilities (SEND) – and this was the game-changer.

What kind of school did you go to? Did it feel **inclusive**?

How did it influence your **personal philosophy** about education?

Was school a **positive or a negative** experience for you?

There was a special school and alternative provision in the city where I was living and, much as I had been deeply passionate about my subject at the start of my career, it soon transpired that working with children and young people with SEND was everything I had gone into teaching for. The school in which I worked was staffed by an amazing, inspiring, and forward-thinking team of individuals who were all reading from the same relational sheet of pedagogy, and were all willing to bend and adapt to the needs of the children and young people. We delivered everything from dog care to core GCSEs, cooking to philosophy and ethics, entry level qualifications to science and humanities. I remember teaching a wonderful young man who would initially sit with a towel in front of his face in his bedroom, who we eventually successfully reintegrated into the school building and who sat and passed all of his GCSEs.

It was a fantastic time, surrounded by fantastic staff and brilliant young people, and it totally tapped into and developed my personal approaches to education. Since those days, I have returned to a mainstream setting but still work within SEND, and do so because I know how challenging it can be as a non-specialist in SEND to be expected to adapt and bend flexibly when you have 30 children in a class, or indeed several sets of 30 if you're in a secondary setting. I made the move back in the hope of supporting staff to achieve this, and hence this book was born. The guidance within the book regarding adapting our teaching and our approaches will be of benefit to all children and young people, because **excellent teaching for pupils with SEND is excellent teaching for all**. Within its pages, the term SEND will be used inclusively and, to also incorporate and mirror inclusion, the views of support staff, teachers, parents, children, site staff, governors – a whole host of stakeholders – have been sought and considered. It focuses on adapting teaching for children with SEND as opposed to, for example, adapting school buildings for those with disabilities, the latter being an area that will be overseen in school by leaders, site managers, and Special Educational Needs and Disabilities Co-ordinators (SENDCOs).

I've been extremely lucky in my career to work with some fantastically skilled, talented and inspiring teachers and support staff. Some have been secondary specialists, some primary, others at the start of their careers, and others at the end. I've worked with a couple of outstanding headteachers whose leadership styles have been grounded in a starting point of emotional literacy and intelligence, and who've inspired me to do the same. I've worked with admin staff who've built better relationships, and have therefore contributed to getting better outcomes for children than experienced teachers have managed. And I've also spoken with people who have worked in schools where leaders have, without necessarily realising, created 'us and them' cultures between staff and young people, resulting in low morale amongst all stakeholders and, most importantly and worryingly, poor outcomes for children.

What this book is about, and what it aims to do, is contribute in some small way to getting those better outcomes for children and young people. What it doesn't aim to do is fire off rounds of blame. None of us gets it right all of the time. We can all think of an example when we have escalated a situation, or we've just been too tired to see the woods for the proverbial, and we've acted in a way that we wish we hadn't. You may be reading this and recognising experiences of your own which have been similar, or even recognising instances where you've messed up or reflected on and regretted something. But that reflection is a positive, that reflection is what we do as teachers to then effect positive change. And that positive change is what it's all about – that's when we get to change the world. Maybe only just a little, maybe just a tiny ripple, but how much better is a tiny ripple than making no difference at all? And if you can spread that little ripple around you to others, then actually the difference that you make becomes huge. You may well be reading and thinking of examples from your own childhood that have made you the person and the teacher that you are today and, in their own way, those examples and your own very personal experiences will now be both influencing and, by proxy, affecting, the children that you teach – and the children they may go on to have, or even teach themselves.

In summary, this book is not about having things done 'to' you, it's about doing things 'with' you. It's about 'us' – as teachers, as people, as individuals – in it together and always trying to make things that bit better.

Who have you been fortunate enough to work with so far in your career?

Is there anyone who **directly changed** the path that your career before and/ or since entering teaching has taken?

Which **colleagues** have inspired you and what was it about them that struck you as inspirational?

Consider yourself – in what ways do **you** inspire others?

A Word About You and Adapting for Yourself

Before we progress any further, we need to talk about the most important person reading this book, and that person is you. Whatever role you currently play in school, you are a key component on which all else rests and, before you can be the best you can be for the children, you need to be the best you can be for yourself.

Teaching is hard. Teaching is exhausting. Just speak to anyone, myself and possibly your own self included, who has had other jobs and can make the comparison legitimately. If not for the holidays, there is every chance that plenty of us could not (note: I do not say would not!) do the job, because we become consumed, and often physically and mentally overwhelmed. I don't say this lightly but I do say it truthfully. You'll know as you're reading this that you cannot switch off from teaching. That you probably arrive at 7/7.30am, stay until 5/5.30pm (excluding performances, parents'/carers' evenings, and so forth), and go home to eat and then continue working. It is unsustainable. The expectations of the job are massive, contributing to the holistic raising, educating, and nurturing of between 30 and several hundred children a week, each with individual needs and circumstances.

You absolutely must look after yourself – put your own oxygen mask on first and all that other metaphorical jazz before you board the plane of education – and you must know and recognise when to slow down, otherwise you may not reach the fabled land of the Great Summer Holiday, the destination where we all descend and refuel, before you crash involuntarily.

Be **honest**, there's nobody here but us teacher types. Do you embrace wellbeing as a concept, or do you eye-roll when you hear it?

What does wellbeing really mean to **you**, personally?

How closely linked is school to your personal wellbeing?

To what extent do you believe the senior leadership team (**SLT**) are responsible for your wellbeing?

Wellbeing

There is much ado about wellbeing in schools currently and long may that continue. We all know that physical exercise, having a nice bath, meeting a friend for coffee, and so on is helpful, but we also need to know when to set our own boundaries. If you help a neighbour with their shopping, or you feel that you should offer to pick up a friend's children when you collect your own, for example, and feed them and occupy them until your friend can arrive, then that's fine all the time that you're feeling able to – that's the way we get through life, via our buddies and favours that we both carry out and repay. But there may be times when you need to say no. There may be times when you get home from school to a mountain of washing or work or cooking, and you have to say no, and sit on the sofa instead. But don't sit there frowning and muttering to yourself that 'no-one else is going to do it', getting back up less than 5 minutes after you sat down to just crack on. Instead, set your boundaries and *do not* feel guilty. Maybe nobody else will do it, but the roof won't fall in if you leave it a day longer, or ignore it until the weekend. Once in a while, selfishness is ok. Once in a while, it's alright to give full and absolute priority to yourself, safe in the recognition that doing so will lead to better outcomes for the children and young people in your care – and for your own family.

What Can You Control?

It is also useful to think about what you can control. This is easier said than done when our to-do list feels as though it runs for miles, but it is helpful. Consider what you can control, what you can partially control, and what you can't control at all – because the latter is where we need to try to care a little less, or better still let go entirely, whilst focusing on what we can do for ourselves. Take the weather, for example. We cannot control the weather, but we can control what clothing we are going to wear to protect ourselves or to feel our most comfortable.

Focusing on the things we can control **empowers** us, and letting go of the things we can't enables us to stop feeling overwhelmed. We cannot control the fact that our subject leader or year group leader expects us to mark all 4 papers of the English GCSE mock, or all 6 SATs practice papers, for myriad students, in a short turnaround period. However, we can control some aspects of this because we know it's coming. We are aware in advance that the assessment-marking train is hurtling straight towards us, and we can either become overwhelmed and just lay on the tracks begging it to do its worst, or we can take control, plan our social life in advance of that period, adjust other aspects of our workload in advance, and adapt for ourselves just as we adapt for the students. And it's really important that we do so. It's all too easy to be told this stuff – or to read it in a book – and then forget it, ignore it, or scoff at it amid our overwhelmed brains shrieking, 'don't they know how busy I am!?' Saying 'be mindful' has a hint of cheese to it for some of us, but it really is useful to keep such advice at the forefront of our minds. To **stop for a moment** and to think about what we can control, to think about setting some boundaries, and to then act on that and get on top of things before they boggle us.

Your school should have a wellbeing or mental health policy, a member of staff (or several) who oversee it, and you should have contacts to speak to or seek support from when you need to. Make sure that you do – adapt for yourself as much as you need to adapt for the students. You are number one here because, much as we are in it for the children, we do have to actually *be in it* for it to work, whereas if you're broken with physical and mental exhaustion, you'll be firmly out! And, as the very premise of this book suggests, we need to be included, not excluded. It's all about inclusion.

What do you **actively** do to look after yourself?

Do you have a support system at school?

Are you able **to share** with friends and family?

Are you able to contribute to wellbeing yourself at school and support others? What might/does that look like?

What Is This 'Inclusion' That You Speak Of?

What Does 'Inclusion' Mean to You?

It makes sense for us to have a look at this because if you're building your inclusive class-room, with that foundation of relational approaches, then we need to decipher what an inclusive classroom is.

You may work in a setting where the SENDCO is also the inclusion lead. Alternatively, you may work in a school where an entirely different member of staff is leading on inclusion. Either way, what these staff members will often have in common, is that they will be members of the SLT. This is because if these folk are on the SLT, then they have more ability to steer and elicit positive strategic change for children and young people. Obviously, plenty of headteachers will listen to their SENDCO whether they are on the SLT or not, and that's what really matters. After all, you may be a SENDCO reading this who is, for example, an assistant headteacher, but who doesn't feel listened to at all so, in reality, much rests upon the headteacher and their personal approaches and beliefs about SEND.

All of this leads us nicely back to the terminology of 'inclusion' and what it is, because if a school is truly inclusive, then all **stakeholders** should feel listened to, heard, and valued. By 'stakeholders', we mean everyone from the headteacher to the governing body, to the staff, children, parents, and local community. The old adage of 'it takes a village to raise a child' is oft-used and with good reason, perhaps even more so in cur-rent times. Essentially, the whole-school vision for inclusion is for our senior leaders to decide, whilst bearing in mind the needs of the school and community, and we then play our parts in building and embedding this. Our classrooms are subcommunities within the broader community of the school, and if you're a class teacher, you can contribute to and play your part in the wider scheme of things by, in the main, ensuring that your own classroom, your own teaching space, is inclusive. So, what does this mean? What does it look like?

A definition of 'inclusion' itself, at its most basic, means being included, but it is so much more complex than this. We can all tell someone that they have **been** included, but surely what makes the difference is **feeling** included? Whether you have 100 children in your school or 2000 children, ensuring that each of those children experiences the **feeling** of inclusion – as well as all other stakeholders – is immense, and nigh on impossible. However, as with much in teaching, we keep trying and we keep adapting. For the majority of children and young people, tutors, assemblies, lessons, breaktimes, extra-curricular clubs, friend-ships, and so forth, all provide the feeling of inclusion. For others, whether because of par-ticular needs or life circumstances, they do not, and this may be where some extra thought and support are needed.

Our SENDCOs should make clear their vision for inclusion of children with SEND (more on this later in the chapter), and then put in place particular strategies and plans in order to provide support that will ensure it, but the core of this will be what happens in the class-room and how we adapt our teaching and our approaches to ensure that all children are able to access their learning, and that all children therefore feel included in it.

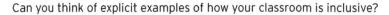

What definition would you now give of '**inclusion**'?

What would your personal vision of inclusion for your **classroom** be?

Can you think of explicit examples of how your classroom is inclusive?

Can you think of examples of when your classroom has not been as inclusive as you'd like, and how you could **change** that?

The Model for Your Inclusive Classroom

Now that we've considered inclusion in more detail, let's look again at the blueprint from the introduction regarding how to build your inclusive classroom. This will be referred to throughout the book and considered in further depth at the start of Chapter 3 (Figure 1.1)

In essence, the foundation of your classroom should be *immoveable*. Your classroom needs to stand on solid ground, and that groundwork should be comprised of **relational approaches**. These, and the reasons for them, will be discussed in depth during Chapters 3 and 4.

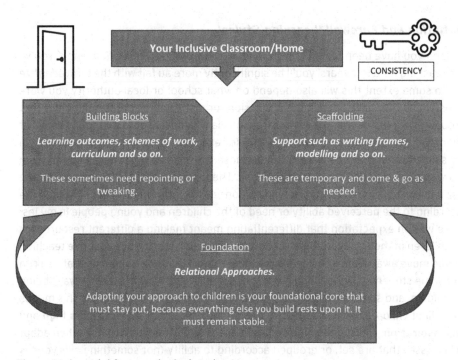

Figure 1.1 A model for your inclusive classroom

The key to your inclusive classroom is **consistency** – consistently high expectations and consistently high quality teaching. Your building blocks and scaffolding can come and go as needed, with your recognising this, and adapting where required. Chapters 5 and 6 in particular, when we look at methods of **adaptive teaching**, will provide excellent ideas on how to do so.

By following this blueprint, we can aim high. We can aim to build a classroom where all learners are known, valued, included, and where they also *feel* this. Where they are safe, where they can achieve, and where they are heard. We can aim for, and we can achieve, inclusion.

Adaptive Teaching or Differentiation?

Do you know these terms and the differences between them?

Given that this book is based upon the core concept of adapting our teaching and our approaches to meet the needs within our classrooms and schools, it seems appropriate to begin with a word or several about the terminology that is currently in use and the differences between these approaches. 'Adaptive teaching' is that which is being moved towards, and 'differentiation' is a little more old-skool.

Differentiation and Farewell 'Learning Styles'

However long you have been teaching, you will have heard of *differentiation*, and if you've only been teaching for a few years, you'll be significantly more au fait with the term *adaptive teaching*. To some extent this will also depend on what school or local authority you work in. For those of us who have been in the profession for many years, 'differentiation' is that which probably haunted us throughout our training via whichever route we took to arrive at destination: teacher. When I was doing my PGCE for example, I had to write a detailed plan for every single lesson that I delivered, and on those plans was a box where I had to fill in whether I was differentiating via outcome or task. The former meant that everyone did the same task and I was prepared for a variety of responses, the latter meant that I changed the tasks according to the perceived ability or need of the children and young people in my lessons. There was an expectation that differentiating meant making a different resource for different children in the class – in some schools, this may still stand – but adaptive teaching is a welcome move away from it. Aside from adding to workload, it also means that you run the risk of some students always being given the 'low ability task', with others always being given the middle, and some always receiving the high. Falling into patterns like this means that we can limit children, whereas what we need to do is keep our **expectations high** and encourage **aspiration**, whilst gauging changes in needs and attainment that we then adapt to. Even in classes that are set, or grouped according to ability (not something everyone is keen on), each child is, of course, different. And this is why adaptation is so crucial.

Back in those olden days of my PGCE, I also had to fill in a box entitled 'VAK', which stood for Visual, Auditory and Kinaesthetic, and in this box I had to explicitly state how my resources would account for these 3 types of 'learning style'. I had to have pupils moving about or engaged in something practical, whilst ensuring that there was something auditory for pupils who were considered to learn by hearing or sound, and furthermore planning something visual, such as image enquiries and the like. To be fair, what this approach did do was force one to think creatively about what was being presented in the classroom, but it also caused untold anxiety as a student to try and ensure that I was identifying all learning styles in the room and making corresponding resources for everyone in it, and then providing written reflections afterwards regarding how successful (or otherwise) I had been in doing so. Again, as with producing 3 or more different worksheets, the issue here is that we cannot categorise students into particular little learning boxes and there they shall stay. We end up pigeonholing students, lowering our expectations without meaning to, and probably lowering the students' expectations of themselves to boot.

I am pleased to say that such theory regarding learning style has since been **debunked**. As Paul Kirschner, a cognitive psychologist, suggests, having a preferred method of study does not equate to a learning style and, also, there is a real difference between the *way* in which someone prefers to learn, versus *actually learning* effectively, in a manner that leads to progress (Kirschner 2016). Therefore, do not assign your students 'learning styles': keep your mind open and, in doing so, keep the learning opportunities open for all students. What we actually need to do is adapt our methods depending on what we see the children learning or not learning, thereby addressing this to then make progress.

How well do you **know** your students and their needs?

How **long** does it take you to get to know your students?

If you teach in a primary setting, how does your knowledge of the students in September compare to that in December? And how does this then **affect the adaptations** that you make?

If you teach in a secondary setting and see the students less frequently, how can you get to know them and their needs as swiftly and efficiently as possible? Who might you speak to? Whose support might you seek?

Adaptive Teaching

Fast forward 20 years (and it really has felt fast, much as that may seem unlikely if you're just starting out and some days resemble years), and things have changed – for the better. In the **Early Career Framework** (ECF), the term 'adaptive teaching' appeared in 2019, and is the fifth standard that Early Career Teachers (ECTs) are expected to meet. This is a step away from the expectation of making umpteen different resources for umpteen different students, and a move towards adapting learning in manageable but still impactful ways.

Differentiation as a term has the connotations of making and printing a variety of worksheets; *adaptive teaching* is suggestive instead of maintaining high expectations whilst – and this is key – **knowing** your pupils and then, for example, reframing questions accordingly, and linking new content to prior learning. In fact, the ECF states explicitly that 'adaptive teaching is less likely to be valuable if it causes the teacher to artificially create distinct tasks for different groups of pupils or to set lower expectations for particular pupils' (Early Career Framework 2019). This approach is joy to the ears of those who trained under the VAK regime. Instead, it is acknowledged that in order to best teach children with (and without) SEND, we must do so with rigour, with robust high expectations, and in a manner that is adapted to their needs.

Getting to know our pupils, who they are and what makes them tick, and getting to know them as learners, means that we give them the best learning experiences that they can get. As teachers, we have to bend and adapt flexibly in order to engage our students as best we can, and to therefore support them in achieving the very best that they can.

At the risk of breaking out into a 1980s power ballad, the children in our classes are the future of our world, developing in front of our very eyes. There may well be times when this thought fills us with deep concern for the survival of humanity, such as when we look around, stunned, scanning the carnage at 3pm on a Friday and engaging in dark mutterings with ourselves. But isn't this concern, and the wish to counteract it, exactly the thing that drives us? The thing that can motivate us just as much as the unexpected joy of discovering one solitary teenager who actually believes it's relevant to study Shakespeare in the 21st century?

It's a tall order, for sure, but it's teaching. That's the reality of the profession. For the folk out there who appear to loathe us, and who waggle their little pitchforks of judgment at every opportunity in the comments section of some newspapers, I say join the profession for a week. Learn about the lack of funding, the amount of planning, the wads of paperwork, the number of meetings, the parents' evenings, the residential trips and policies, inspections, observations (I could go on) – before even getting into a classroom. Basically, unless one has been a teacher, and has also engaged in a variety of other professions for comparison, then it's nonsense to indulge in such judgmental speculation.

In many ways, the statistics speak for themselves. In 2021, 12.5% of ECTs left teaching before their careers even really got started (Belger 2022). What an incredibly sad and concerning statistic – and what a red flag pointing towards how tough it can be. However, despite the challenges (or maybe because of them, and how fantastic it feels when you overcome them) teaching is more than a little bit magical. You'll know what I'm talking about; those lessons that are simply incendiary, the ones where you leave on an absolute high – as do the children – because you've created *memorable learning experiences* that may stay with those young people for the rest of their lives and shape the adults that they go on to become. Lessons where you see that 9-year-old who has been struggling with maths suddenly having a life-changing lightbulb moment when the link between fractions and percentages just clicks. Or when the teenager who gave you explicit instructions on what to do with yourself on Monday, whilst using which implements, seeks you out off their own back on Friday to apologise. That's what teaching is truly about, those moments of pure magic, so let's keep them firmly at the forefront of our minds – and adaptive teaching makes the load a little easier, so let's look at it in more detail.

What you know of the Early Career Framework will depend on your position in school and how long you've been teaching.

Have you read any of the ECF?

If you've been in teaching for a while, how does the ECF compare to when you were a Newly Qualified Teacher (NQT)?

ECTs now complete a 2-year induction period as opposed to the one year of NQTs. Is this a positive? What difference, if any, might this make?

If we cast an eye in the direction of the Early Career Framework, because the advice is clear and relevant to all teachers regardless of experience, then according to Standard 5, we need to **know that**:

1. Pupils are likely to learn at different rates and to require different levels and types of support from teachers to succeed.
2. Seeking to understand pupils' differences, including their different levels of prior knowledge and potential barriers to learning, is an essential part of teaching.
3. Adapting teaching in a responsive way, including by providing targeted support to pupils who are struggling, is likely to increase pupil success.
4. Adaptive teaching is less likely to be valuable if it causes the teacher to artificially create distinct tasks for different groups of pupils or to set lower expectations for particular pupils.
5. Flexibly grouping pupils within a class to provide more tailored support can be effective, but care should be taken to monitor its impact on engagement and motivation, particularly for low attaining pupils.
6. There is a common misconception that pupils have distinct and identifiable learning styles. This is not supported by evidence and attempting to tailor lessons to learning styles is unlikely to be beneficial.
7. Pupils with special educational needs or disabilities are likely to require additional or adapted support; working closely with colleagues, families, and pupils to understand barriers and identify effective strategies is essential.

Furthermore, we need to know **how to:**

Develop an understanding of different pupil needs, by:

- Identifying pupils who need new content further broken down.
- Making use of formative assessment.
- Working closely with the Special Educational Needs Co-ordinator (SENCO) and special education professionals and the Designated Safeguarding Lead.
- Using the SEND Code of Practice, which provides additional guidance on supporting pupils with SEND effectively.

Provide opportunity for all pupils to experience success, by:

- Adapting lessons, whilst maintaining high expectations for all, so that all pupils have the opportunity to meet expectations.
- Balancing input of new content so that pupils master important concepts.
- Making effective use of teaching assistants.

Meet individual needs without creating unnecessary workload, by:

- Use of well-designed resources (e.g. textbooks).
- Planning to connect new content with pupils' existing knowledge or providing additional pre-teaching if pupils lack critical knowledge.
- Building in additional practice or removing unnecessary expositions.
- Reframing questions to provide greater scaffolding or greater stretch.

We can see here, explicitly, that adaptive teaching acknowledges that we do not need to, and should not, create different tasks for different groups of children, that we do not have to identify and plan for different 'learning styles', and that we should in fact respond and adapt our teaching to the whole class, and not the pigeonholes that we can sometimes unwittingly create.

Let's return then to a premise from earlier in the chapter because, much as this book leans towards teaching children with SEND, excellent teaching for those students really is excellent teaching for all. In turn, adaptive teaching is excellent teaching. Therefore, if we adapt said teaching for whole classes, then we **achieve inclusion** for all learners.

CHAPTER 1: MEETING NEEDS

Takeaways

- This book is about **inspiration!**
- **Relationships,** and knowing a bit about each other, are crucial to the success of everyone in the classroom and the school …

- ... including you, so look after **yourself**.
- Relational approaches are the **foundation** of our inclusive classroom.
- Adaptive teaching is not the same as differentiation. It is more **responsive**.
- We must never pigeonhole students and must maintain **high expectations**.
- We can build an inclusive classroom whereby **all learners** feel included in their learning, and we can contribute to a whole-school vision of inclusion by embedding this.

COMING UP NEXT

- **Chapter 2** is going to look at how we should speak about SEND, the 4 Broad Areas of SEND, Neurodiversity, being needs-led as opposed to diagnosis-led, legally binding support plans for children and young people with SEND, and the role of the SENDCO. We'll also consider a model of Cause and Effect for helping us to meet the needs of children.

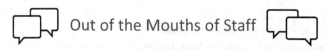 Out of the Mouths of Staff

I loved school and I loved my teachers. I admired them and although I came into teaching later, I realised that a career in teaching would be much more satisfying. I had always been in Guiding and was a Guide Leader and soon realised that I had a bit of a way with young adults which led me into seniors.

Deputy Head and Inclusion Lead, Secondary

For me, inclusion means everyone being able to access provision that is appropriate to them and does not exclude them. It means including the most vulnerable pupils in the school and meeting their needs.

Headteacher, Primary

Personally, I believe inclusion means creating an environment in which difference is celebrated and accepted. Inclusion is ensuring all children can access learning, whatever their additional needs (including if they do not have SEND). It is about adapting learning and expectations to and for our learners. Helping them to feel accepted and celebrated, supporting them to thrive.

Humanities Teacher, Secondary

Growing up, I always knew I wanted to work with people but one experience of a teacher changed my life. I have a specific learning difficulty – a mix of dyspraxia and dyslexia which brings with it very poor working memory. My Geography GCSE teacher's style of teaching was to stand at the front of the class and dictate out of a textbook. For someone with very poor processing speed and working memory this was barely accessible. However, I worked extremely hard and found the content interesting so when considering my A Level choices, I decided to do Geography. This time, I had the most amazing and inspiring teacher who made my lessons engaging. It made me realise if one teacher could make such a difference to me then it was a worthwhile profession to be in.

Subject Leader, Geography

When I was a student, we were taught that children had different learning styles. It seems ludicrous now because this places limits on students. Effective learning takes place in lots of different ways for everyone. It's about recognising that and then teaching effectively, adapting what we're doing to meet the needs of all students. It's not about saying that Timmy only learns through visual stimulus and Leroy only learns by listening.

Headteacher, Primary

References

Belger, T. (2022). *Jump in Teachers Leaving*. Available at: https://schoolsweek.co.uk/dfe-teacher-vacancy-pay-jobs-recruitment-data/

Department for Education and Department of Health. (2019). *Early Career Framework*. Available at: https://assets.publishing.service.gov.uk/government/uploads/system/uploads/attachment_data/file/978358/Early-Career_Framework_April_2021.pdf (Accessed: 10 July 2023).

Kirschner, P. (2016). Stop Propagating the Learning Styles Myth. *Computers & Education*, 106, pp. 166–171. http://doi.org/10.1016/j.compedu.2016.12.006.

The Early Career Framework: DFE-00015-2019.

Chapter Two

What Are Special Educational Needs and/ or Disabilities (SEND)?

Chapter 2	A Summary
What Are SEND?	A delve into how we, as teachers, learn about SEND, and how to **talk** about SEND. We'll look at the 4 Broad Areas of SEND, **neurodiversity**, being **needs-led as opposed to diagnosis-led**, and all about **legally-binding plans** of support for children and young people with SEND such as Education, Health, and Care Plans (EHCPs) in England or Individual Development Plans (IDPs) in Wales and so on. We'll also look at a model of **Cause and Effect** for supporting needs, and consider what the Special Educational Needs and/or Disabilities Co-ordinator (**SENDCO**) does in schools - the only member of school staff who is required to be educated to Master's Level and hold qualified teacher status (QTS).

When Do Teachers Get Taught About SEND?

Depending on what path one takes into teaching, it can be a bit of a rollercoaster ride with a lot of learning on the job, and it's usually - in the grand scheme of things - a relatively speedy process. One day, we are watching others teach and possibly thinking that 'this looks ok, I can do this'. The next, we are having a sweaty awakening in front of 30 beady-eyed, highly observant children or young people, realising that it only looked OK before because we couldn't feel the tensions underneath the class, much less control those tensions like a seasoned conductor.

Whatever route into teaching you have taken, it is unlikely, due to time constraints and so forth, that you spent a vast amount of time being taught about SEND (sometimes, depending on where one works, referred to under different names - such as Additional Learning Needs, or ALN, in Wales for example - but essentially the same thing). Universities and teacher training programmes have certainly made huge progress in this area, with some sending their trainees for a week or 2 into special schools or Alternative/additional Provisions (AP), but the scope of SEND is so vast - because the differences between us as human beings is so vast - that the majority of our learning has to be on the job. Of course, on the job is when we are then at our busiest, and so time constraints again are a limitation.

DOI: 10.4324/b23417-3

Many teachers will know about the **SEND Code of Practice**, which is statutory guidance, but few will have read it cover to cover if they are teaching within mainstream provision, and nor will they need to. However, as the Early Career Framework (ECF) tells us, we do have to have a working knowledge of it, or use it for reference. The Code of Practice states that, **'every teacher is a teacher of SEND'**, meaning that it is our responsibility as class teachers to ensure that children with additional needs are taught robustly, with high expectations, and that we adapt our practice and our approaches accordingly (Special Educational Needs and Disability Code of Practice: 0-25 Years, 2015). The Code of Practice also talks about 'high-quality teaching' which, hopefully, is what we all strive for.

What **provision** about SEND was there when you were training to teach?

Have you met colleagues that had a different experience whilst training?

Does your school provide **training** around SEND? Have other schools you've worked in provided more or less? Why was that?

If you have any SEND yourself, **how** were those supported whilst you were training? How are you supported in school now?

How Should We Speak About SEND?

If for any reason you feel daunted by asking a child or their family about their preferences when referring to their needs, ask your SENDCO for advice.

Before we go further in looking at SEND, it's worth discussing the language that we use around it. You may have noted that I write about 'children with SEND' rather than 'SEND children'. It's important not to define a child by, for example, their emotional needs. However, inclusive language and the advice around it is constantly evolving, and the best and most important thing that you can do, is to ask the child and their family for their preference - this is **inclusion**. In terms of your own professional development, it is worth investigating inclusive language every so often to ensure that you're up to date (and hopefully your SENDCO does so for you).

In the autistic community, according to, for example, the National Autistic Society, many autistic people see their autism as being a core and fundamental part of who they are, and the use of identity-first language is advised, such as saying **'autistic child/person/adult'**. They also suggest that when referring to a specific person then the best thing to do is to ask them for their preference - and that this preference should take precedent over anyone else's guidance regarding how to speak about autism. Do not be afraid to do so; this is inclusive. It's about being person-centred and person-led, and it goes to show the importance of our **really knowing** the children in our classroom.

You may work in a school where there is a WhatsApp group or maybe a coffee morning group for parents of children with SEND, and those parents may choose to refer to themselves as 'SEND parents/carers' – this choice can be empowering for parents. With some students, especially as they get older, you'll notice that they may have preferred ways in which to refer to themselves or their needs. It's empowering for us as humans to exercise our choice and have our voices heard and our personal opinions valued, and that is key to SEND. Again, this links also to what we can control and what we can't, and choosing how we are described or referred to, is a basic but important right. We can effect positive change for inclusion by being mindful of the terminology that we use, and we should aim to do this in our classrooms.

This all links into the relational practice that we'll examine in Chapters 3 and 4 because, ideally, your relationships with students will be strong, you'll be putting them at the centre of all, and you can ask them for their preferences so that you won't inadvertently cause offence. If you are only at the start of a conversation and have not yet had the chance to check on preferences, then it can also be helpful to listen closely to how individuals refer to themselves and then mirror that language.

Inappropriate Language

In times gone by, some very uncomfortable language has been used about people with SEND. Disappointingly of course this still happens now – even the word 'special' is taken by some and used in a derogatory manner. But previously, even governments did so, when particular words that we would now consider to be deeply inappropriate were regarded as simply standard. Examples of this include the excruciatingly named 'Idiots Act' of 1886, which was an act of Parliament detailing the admission of 'idiots and imbeciles into training institutions'. This is morally **repugnant**. It is deeply emotive that terminology such as 'ineducable' was in frequent public use until the 1980s and beyond in some instances, and it is worth remembering that from these beginnings, our current terminology was born.

It can be worth **discussing our language** around SEND with our colleagues. If you hear something inappropriate, would you feel comfortable in politely addressing it? How would you do so?

Does your SENDCO **address language** around SEND at school and give guidance and advice?

Have you read your school's **policy** for SEND?

When I consider some of the fabulous children I have taught, and still teach, it's unbearable to imagine the past language of SEND as ever having been seen as remotely appropriate, and this is another reason why children and young people with SEND need advocates. If we consider ourselves as adults being referred to in the workplace in such terms, it is unimaginable. If we then go a step further and consider the damage that such labelling would do to one's self-esteem – not to mention the effect on public perceptions and opinions of us were those terms to be in frequent use and advocated by those in authority – then it's simply unthinkable; abhorrent. We must therefore be mindful of what we *say* as well as what we *do*. Even as adults it can be hard to stand up for ourselves, and so we must also support young people in becoming their own self-advocates – listen to them, encourage them, empower them.

Many aspects of our roles as teachers are complex, but we do go into the profession to make the fabled difference, so one of the best things we can do for ourselves and our own job satisfaction, is to ensure that we've done our best for the children. This consideration of language spans far and wide when building an inclusive classroom for all children, whether they have SEND or not, for example:

Example:	Consider using instead:
Joey had a complete meltdown	Joey became heightened
Arhem totally lost it, he has no idea how to behave	We are supporting Arhem with his self-regulation which he finds difficult
EHCP (Education, Health, and Care Plan) children	Children with an EHCP
Deficient/deficiency	Difference
Holly is clueless about the impact of their behaviour	We are supporting Holly with their self-awareness
Our LAC students	Our students who are Looked After Children
Harlow is attention-seeking	Harlow is seeking connection

Now that we have discussed a little on the topic of the language that we use to build inclusivity, it is worth highlighting that it would be a huge and unrealistic expectation to believe that all teachers working in mainstream schools will have detailed knowledge about all aspects of SEND and different forms of SEND. Even those working in specialist provisions have to research and refresh in order to ensure we understand the needs of individuals.

The absolute best thing we can really do when we are directly at the chalkface is to **get to know the children** – observe them learning, try new things, chat with them, ask them about their needs and what they find helpful – and do it in a way that ensures they are comfortable. It's also helpful to speak with their parents or carers, who are usually more than happy to be listened to and to engage in getting the best support they can for their child. Adaptive teaching, as opposed to the old-style, time-consuming differentiation of yesteryear, means that it's actually that bit easier to reach those heady heights of 'best' without having to spend all day and night planning.

So, you do not need to have an encyclopaedic knowledge of all aspects of SEND to teach and support children successfully, but you do have to know the child, know what their individual needs mean for them, and adapt to this. But, whatever the need, we must avoid pigeonholing children according to those needs, just as we must avoid grouping children into specific learning styles.

Do you feel nervous about **'getting it wrong'**? What makes you nervous – or not?

Have you ever discussed this with a colleague, or perhaps seen a colleague or heard one say that they've inadvertently caused offence?

In an age of 'cancel culture' we can feel real fear sometimes in our classrooms. Take the lead from your students and their families – follow their own preferences and advice. They are your best source of how to get things right.

The 4 Broad Areas of SEND

Generally, you will probably hear about SEND as being divided into 4 areas of need, although there is much overlap here. It is within the SEND Code of Practice (full reference at the end of this chapter) that we find these, and they are:

Broad Area of Need	What the SEND Code of Practice Tells Us
Communication and Interaction	6.28 – Children and young people with Speech, Language and Communication Needs (SLCN) have difficulty in communicating with others. This may be because they have difficulty saying what they want to, understanding what is being said to them, or they do not understand or use social rules of communication. The profile for every child with SLCN is different and their needs may change over time. They may have difficulty with one, some or all of the different aspects of speech, language or social communication at different times of their lives. 6.29 – Children and young people with Autistic Spectrum Condition (ASC), including Asperger's Syndrome and Autism, are likely to have particular difficulties with social interaction. They may also experience difficulties with language, communication, and imagination, which can impact on how they relate to others.
Cognition and Learning	6.30 – Support for learning difficulties may be required when children and young people learn at a slower pace than their peers, even with appropriate differentiation. Learning difficulties cover a wide range of needs, including Moderate Learning Difficulties (MLD), Severe Learning Difficulties (SLD), where children are likely to need support in all areas of the curriculum and associated difficulties with mobility and communication, through to Profound and Multiple Learning Difficulties (PMLD), where children are likely to have severe and complex learning difficulties as well as a physical disability or sensory impairment. 6.31 – Specific Learning Difficulties (SpLD) affect one or more specific aspects of learning. This encompasses a range of conditions such as dyslexia, dyscalculia, and dyspraxia.

Social, Emotional, and Mental Health (SEMH)	6.32 – Children and young people may experience a wide range of social and emotional difficulties which manifest themselves in many ways. These may include becoming withdrawn or isolated, as well as displaying challenging, disruptive or disturbing behaviour. These behaviours may reflect underlying mental health difficulties such as anxiety or depression, self-harming, substance misuse, eating disorders or physical symptoms that are medically unexplained. Other children and young people may have disorders such as attention deficit disorder, attention deficit hyperactive disorder or attachment disorder. 6.33 – Schools and colleges should have clear processes to support children and young people, including how they will manage the effect of any disruptive behaviour so it does not adversely affect other pupils.
Sensory and Physical Needs	6.34 – Some children and young people require special educational provision because they have a disability which prevents or hinders them from making use of the educational facilities generally provided. These difficulties can be age-related and may fluctuate over time. Many children and young people with Vision Impairment (VI), Hearing Impairment (HI), or Multi-Sensory Impairment (MSI) will require specialist support and/or equipment to access their learning, or habilitation support. Children and young people with an MSI have a combination of vision and hearing difficulties. 6.35 – Some children and young people with a physical disability (PD) require additional ongoing support and equipment to access all the opportunities available to their peers.

It is helpful for class teachers to have a broad overview such as this so that we can build our inclusive classrooms with this layer of knowledge in our minds for reference, and to therefore be in a position to identify possible needs. Clearly, there is huge variation within these areas. Not all SEND are permanent, and some children and young people may have needs in more than one of these areas. Some SEND may be lifelong – particularly some disabilities, for example.

When it comes to you knowing exactly what a child's specific needs are and what you can do to support their learning in an impactful and meaningful manner, then your SENDCO is your port of call, but do bear in mind that it is also your responsibility to identify if there may be a child with unidentified needs in your classroom. Not every child who struggles to make progress in your class has SEND, but do raise any concerns with your SENDCO – your school will most likely have a system and a policy for doing so. You may notice, for example, a child who finds it tricky to attend to a task for long, or who needs you to explain a task several times. You may find that a child asks to be sat nearer to the board, or is squinting at screens or in visual discomfort in certain lights. Again, not all children who make slower progress will have SEND, but your Learning Support Department will be able to help you if you identify a possible need, and they may have a referral system in place that details any flags to look out for. We shall discuss this further when we look at the role of the SENDCO at the end of this chapter.

Do you know the school's system for **raising concerns** around possible SEND?

Are there children in your class or lessons now who **may** have needs?

Why do you suspect this and **how** are you currently supporting those?

How Does Neurodiversity Fit into the 4 Broad Areas of Need?

If we are to build truly inclusive classrooms, then we really can't do so without having some explicit understanding of the term 'neurodiversity' and the terminology of neurodiversity, some of which is new to many teachers.

Neurodiversity as a term was first used by Judy Singer, a sociologist who is on the autistic spectrum, back in the 1990s (neurodiversityhub). It means that rather than being 'deficient' in anything, including neurodevelopment, those of us who are neurodivergent think about and react to the world differently. As the **Autism Education Trust** succinctly and wonderfully puts it, a neurodiverse condition is 'a different way of being, not a deficient way of being'. The definitions that they provide below are helpful in aiding our understanding (bear in mind that language around SEND is constantly evolving – it is always worth checking for the latest guidance):

Neurodivergent	Neurodivergent can be used to describe someone who has a neurodiverse condition, for example, autism. This means their brain processes information differently. An autistic young person could identify as neurodivergent but so could someone who has a diagnosis of Attention Deficit Hyperactivity Disorder (ADHD) or Dyslexia, for example.
Neurotypical	Neurotypical can be used to describe someone not displaying or characterised by autistic or other neurologically atypical patterns of thought or behaviour.
Neurodiversity	Neurodiversity is the idea that the way we think is not always the same and that there are variations among all of us. Instead, this term recognises that all variations of human neurology should be respected as just another way of being, and that neurological differences like autism, ADHD, and Dyslexia are the result of natural variations in our genes.

In your classroom, you will have both children who are neurotypical and children who are neurodivergent – as indeed we have both staff who are neurotypical and staff who are neurodivergent in school. Some examples of variations in neurodiversity include:

- Autistic Spectrum Condition
- Attention Deficit Hyperactivity Disorder
- Dyspraxia
- Dyslexia
- Dyscalculia
- Tourette Syndrome

Do you know how many of the children in your class or lessons are **diagnosed** with a neurodivergent condition such as being autistic?

How do you access the **SEND Register** in your school?

What systems do you have in school for supporting **you** so that you in turn can best support those children with SEND?

Neurodiversity and Diagnoses: What About Being Needs-Led as Opposed to Diagnosis-Led?

Some children in your class will have been diagnosed as having SEND, for example with a neurodivergent condition like autism, and others may present as such but will not have a diagnosis. Either way, it's our responsibility to support whatever needs the child presents with. This is known as being 'needs-led'.

Being needs-led can come in different forms. For example, when I worked in an Alternative Provision, we followed an entirely needs-led curriculum for each child, with learning personalised solely to them and their interests. I planned lessons using Lana Del Rey lyrics to meet learning outcomes usually associated with *Romeo and Juliet* (before then moving on to *Romeo and Juliet*), and it was a pleasure to do so – it met the needs of the young person and engaged them. Had I leapt in with the text of *Romeo and Juliet*, then it would have been received with as much welcome as someone else's verruca plaster attaching itself to your face as you emerge from the deep end at the local pool.

Other examples of being needs-led mean that we are explicitly not being **diagnosis-led,** which leads to our being **timelier** with our in-class adaptive teaching. In essence, we use the same kinds of strategies that we would use for a child who, for example, is diagnosed with ADHD – re-focusing techniques, repetition, checking understanding – for a child who has no diagnosis but presents as though they may have ADHD.

If one were to *wait* for a diagnosis before putting support in place, then we miss the boat to start making a difference, and these days if we are waiting for a diagnosis, then the child may reach pensionable age before they even get one (or we will). Of course, I hyperbolise, but waiting lists for diagnoses are literal years long – in the UK, at least. And the most important thing the school can do is **support the need**, whether there is a diagnosis or not. Of course, some young people and their parents or carers want a diagnosis for peace of mind, or to aid acceptance, or to make sense of things, but putting support in place should never depend on one. Support should always come first.

In one local authority in the south of England, they have moved entirely towards becoming a needs-led city. Teachers who work within SEND have been trained to complete what are known as *Neuro-Developmental Profiles*. These are carried out across the 9 strands of neurodevelopment where applicable, in co-production with the child or young person and their family, and support is then put in place accordingly. Some of that support is within lessons and around school, other aspects include advice for parents at home and ways in which they can provide support – or adaptations – outside of school.

The 9 strands of neurodevelopment are:

- Energy Levels
- Attention and Impulse Control
- Emotion Regulation Ability
- Motor Skills
- Sensory Skills
- Adaptability and Flexibility
- Cognitive Abilities
- Speech and Language

Do you have students whom you believe may be neurodivergent but **do not have a diagnosis**? How are their **needs** then being supported?

We can see from looking at the 9 strands, in conjunction with the previous examples of variation in neurodiversity, how some of these sit within the 4 broad areas of need, as identified by the SEND Code of Practice. Again, as with specific SEND, a class teacher need not have in-depth knowledge of each of these areas, but having some background understanding of them and that they exist, gives you a context so that when you then meet children with needs you have a clearer grasp on what is happening for them, and why they may present as they do. It supports **understanding** and **empathy**, which is key in encouraging us – as busy, sometimes stressed professionals – to ensure that we are doing our best for children and young people who are neurodivergent. It will be your SENDCO who gives you the need-to-know knowledge and the strategies to use that will best help the child but, again, it's your personal knowledge of the child themselves that will really make the meaningful difference.

In your classroom, you will be meeting some fantastic young people who are neurodivergent and if you've been in teaching for a while then you will already know what a pleasure it can be to teach children who have a different take on the world, and who pick up on patterns or concepts that those who are neurotypical may not. Schools are always very good at pointing to public figures who themselves have additional needs and are successful and inspirational, such as Greta Thunberg, who is contributing to changing the world.

Does your Learning Support Department explicitly advocate a needs-led approach?

Do you know what diagnosis waiting times are like in your local authority at present?

Do you have students who are on a waiting list? Have any decided to seek a private diagnosis because of this?

Support Plans for Children with SEND

Education, Health, and Care Plans (EHCPs) and Equivalents

Depending on where you live, and which country you live in, you'll have a slightly different form of support plan for children with SEND than the EHCPs that are in use throughout England. However, there will be key similarities in characteristics along with the core concept that the plan is legally binding. Scotland, for example, has a Co-ordinated Support Plan (CSP), whereas if you are teaching in Wales, you will be more familiar with the ALN system, which issues IDPs. In Northern Ireland, a Statement of SEND is written. Similar documents are in use internationally, such as in the US, where a child may have an Individual Education Programme (IEP) that is more suited to those who are falling behind academically, or, if a child has disabilities, then they may have what is known as a 504 Plan.

Much of your personal knowledge of EHCPs (or indeed IDPs, CSPs, and so forth) will depend on what your current role is, what your experience is, and also your personal circumstances. If you have little understanding of EHCPs then, in a beginners' guide nutshell, they are legally binding and they document the support and the financial funding that a child or young person with SEND is entitled to if their educational setting is unable to meet their requirements without this extra support, hence not all children with SEND require an EHCP.

EHCPs detail the young person's needs, in each of the 4 broad areas (cognition and learning, communication and interaction, SEMH, and sensory and/or physical needs), and they also detail both **long-term** and **short-term outcomes**, the latter of which will support the young person in achieving the former. An EHCP can last up until a person is 25 years old, however, it does not cover time at university. As with all aspects of SEND, the child should be at the centre of the EHCP process, as of course should their family.

Do you know how many children you teach that have an **EHCP or equivalent plan**?

Are you aware of the outcomes and strategies within the plan?

What system does your SENDCO use to support you in knowing this information and how to use it?

How do you monitor the efficacy of the strategies you're using?

If it is deemed that a child requires an EHCP, the request for it is written by the SENDCO. Certain things need to be in place first and it is a lengthy document to complete. Once written, the request is then sent to the Local Authority (LA), who will either agree it or not and, if it is agreed, will draft it and put it in place. Once a year, the EHCP is reviewed and at this point, depending on the systems in your school, you may be asked to give feedback on how the strategies are working and whether the young person is achieving their short-term outcomes.

Different schools monitor EHCPs in different ways. I have found it successful to put in place a **live document** in an online shared area that details the strategies and outcomes, asking staff to respond on the document once per term regarding progress. In senior settings this has proven useful for teachers to see what colleagues are finding is successful in their lessons and vice versa. In primary, it is helpful for both the teacher, the teaching assistant, and the support member of staff if the child has one funded by their EHCP, to give feedback.

Whatever systems your school implements to monitor the EHCPs or plans of different students, it will be your SENDCO or learning support staff who make you aware of any students with the plans, and who also let you know what it is you need to do in order to support the student. However, don't feel tied to those strategies alone – this is all about getting to really **know** the young people, and through your adaptive teaching you may well find ways of working that are highly supportive and successful, that other staff have not yet tried or thought of.

An example from the SEMH section of an EHCP for a primary-aged child may be:

Social, Emotional, and Mental Health		
Special Educational Need	Outcomes – Long and Medium Term	Interventions and Strategies
Bai becomes distressed during transitions when the routine does not go as expected; he finds change difficult and can become anxious and confused, and then worries about catching up with what he thinks he has missed. Bai will often say he is happy even when he is upset; he has a limited understanding of emotions. He finds it difficult to share and take turns; he struggles with group activities as he likes to take charge and assign roles to others.	Develop his ability to identify a range of emotions within himself (with support) and take active steps to manage this. Take part in small group activities beginning with 1 or 2 peers with adult support, and gradually increase to develop turn-taking skills and sharing.	Provide Bai with ELSA support once a week for 30 minutes, on a 1:1 basis, to help him develop his understanding of where in his body he might feel different emotions (e.g. by completing a body map of where he feels anger/fear/joy/excitement, etc., so that he is able to start to recognise the early warning signs for himself, and later model with him possible ways of managing this by getting him to rate them in terms of their effectiveness). **A teaching assistant will:** Provide Bai with a feelings diary throughout the school day to encourage him to think about how he feels, and draw the event that may have led to this. Support Bai with taking part in structured rule-based games in the playground, supervised by adults who are encouraging him to develop these skills and integrate successfully with his peers (1:4 small group support).

As we can see, much of the onus of this EHCP exemplar rests upon support staff – but as class teacher, you would be expected to ensure that this happening.

Below, we can also see an example of a secondary-aged child's EHCP, in the area of Communication and Interaction:

Communication and Interaction		
Special Educational Need	Outcomes - Long and Medium Term	Interventions and Strategies
Ralphie presents with a severe delay in his attention and listening, understanding and use of language, as well as severe difficulties with his social communication skills. His needs are thought to be long term. He struggles to answer questions about people or events outside the current context. He has difficulty in answering abstract questions that are unrelated to concrete materials. Ralphie is unable to understand 3-step instructions independently. Ralphie will not ask others to expand on things that they have said. In class and on a 1:1 level, he can struggle with word finding and, in addition, will miss out vital words from his sentences. Ralphie refers to himself in the 3rd person when sharing news.	**By the end of Year 9, Ralphie will be able to:** Verbalise his thoughts and ideas using a wide range of vocabulary. Attend to, and follow, a set of instructions with 2 or more steps. **In order to make progress towards this, Ralphie will:** Describe his ideas using a wider range of vocabulary. Identify the key pieces of information in an instruction with 2 steps.	**All staff will:** Provide a highly visual classroom and curriculum for Ralphie. In all lessons, offer concrete resources to help with his word finding abilities (e.g. words mats that contain lists of synonyms for high frequency words such as 'said'). These will be subject specific (e.g. a separate mat for maths which contains shape vocabulary and vocabulary relating to mathematical operations). Allow Ralphie time to find the vocabulary he is searching for by explaining a concept (e.g. size, quality etc.) before prompting him. Provide him with a personalised dictionary that he can add these words to for future reference. Give Ralphie verbal instructions that are broken down into small steps which contain one key piece of information at a time. Ask Ralphie to repeat back instructions before he carries out a task to ensure he understands. If he is being asked to not do something, emphasise this with vocal tones or a gesture. Extend Ralphie's vocabulary by repeating back his sentences and adding a word on. Repeat back Ralphie's sentences so that he can hear the language, especially the sentences he says with words missing, and check with him that they have understood him correctly. **A Teaching Assistant will:** Provide 10 minutes of 1:1 support twice weekly to practise Ralphie's language skills. This will be through the use of short games before he begins his class work, or in between tasks to break up the pace of the lessons. Ideas might include asking Ralphie to think of as many different words that can be used instead of

Communication and Interaction		
Special Educational Need	Outcomes – Long and Medium Term	Interventions and Strategies
		'walking', or asking him to follow a set of instructions where he has to listen closely in order to succeed (e.g. find a shape that is not a square or yellow). These can be turn-taking games where Ralphie competes against himself and his previous scores. Work with Ralphie for 10 minutes per day, on a 1:1 basis, to work on any communication targets that have been identified through his support plan.

When we consider that this is merely a snippet of an EHCP, we begin to get some idea of just how in-depth these documents are due to how much support they must cover and how comprehensive they must be. It is easy to feel daunted looking at this because there is such an onus on us as class teachers to ensure we are delivering on what the EHCP is effectively, and legally, promising. However, do not be daunted! As we shall see when we look further at adaptive teaching and strategies for doing so, much of what you see in that strategy column will become second nature to you.

It's also crucial to use your **support staff** effectively – we can see that Ralphie has some 1:1 support and you must work in conjunction with that teaching or learning support assistant (TA/LSA or similar). We shall look in more depth at this in Chapter 7 but suffice to say that, at the very least, it's good practice to avoid talking to the student through the TA. This may well sound obvious, but I would not say this if I had not witnessed it, nor been told by many support staff across the years that if a student has access to a TA, then sometimes teachers 'forget' the child and just allow the TA to get on with it. This goes against all that inclusion stands for, but when faced with a class of 30, it's easy to forget. However, because you have had the care to even pick up a book such as this and begin reading about what we can do to ensure all children and young people are included in their own learning journeys, then it's clear that you're already striving to provide the best you can for your students.

How do you currently make the most **effective** use of support staff?

Do you welcome them into your room?

Do you know their names?

Can you identify ways in which your use of support staff could be even more effective for both the student and for your relationship with the staff member?

Other Support Plans

For children with SEND who do not require an ECHP, and whose needs can be met through high-quality teaching or interventions, then there are other documents that SENDCOs produce to detail needs and strategies. These come under a variety of names, such as Pen Portraits, or Individual Education Plans (not to be confused with the American equivalent of an EHCP!), Individual Learning Plans, Pupil Passports, and so forth. All will contain details of the young person's needs with strategies for class teachers to support those needs in lessons and around school. These are not legally binding and do not necessitate extra funding, but are ways of ensuring that we know the needs of the children in front of us. In Chapter 6, once we've got some learning about SEND, relational approaches, and adaptive teaching under our belts, we'll take a look at 2 such plans so that you can see how you'd support those children using the knowledge and understanding you've gained from Chapters 1–5.

A Model for Meeting Needs

Cause and Effect

Now that we know more about SEND, it is worth holding in your mind the principle of **cause and effect** throughout this book, known to be a key concept in science (and dominoes), but also helpful to us in supporting our pedagogical thinking around *meeting needs*. Consider the model shown in Figure 2.1.

Identifying those **causes** (unmet needs) of the **effects** that we see in our classrooms (disengagement, gaps in learning and so forth), helps us to then meet those needs, to support them, and to *effect positive change*. As we move through the book, bear this in mind, because we will see it and use it time and time again. It doesn't mean we'll always find a cause, but we should at least *try*.

> Can you think now of any '**effects**' that you are seeing in your lessons, and then consider what the '**cause**' of those might be?
>
> If you identify the cause, how can you support it to effect positive change?
>
> Can you remember a time when you have successfully played a part in doing so?

Find Your SENDCO and Love Them Hard!

At the very epicentre of much that we've discussed in this chapter is, of course, the SENDCO, possibly one of the hardest roles in a school. The SENDCO is the person who elicits strategic change. They are also the person who teachers often perceive as pestering them endlessly with suggestions as to who needs to be taught how, and why. However, they are also a fount of knowledge, of understanding, and they are key to inclusion. The SENDCO is also the only person on the school staff who must be educated to Master's Level (completing their NASENCO qualification within 3 years of commencing

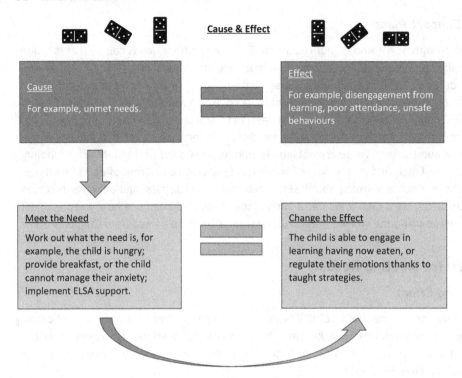

Figure 2.1 A model of Cause and Effect in the classroom

the role), and they must have Qualified Teacher Status (QTS). Interestingly, the headteacher needn't. Who'd have thought!

Very often, mainstream staff assume that SENDCOs work directly and intensively with children with SEND, but as the title suggests, what they more often do is **co-ordinate the support**. There would not be the hours in the year for the SENDCO to work directly with all children who have SEND. Instead, they support everyone else in doing so because schools take a graduated approach to SEND and it all begins with, as the Code of Practice tells us, **high-quality teaching**. This links us back to our central tenet that good, adaptive teaching for children with SEND, is good adaptive teaching for all.

SENDCOs are crucial advocates for all of our children with SEND, and they play a key role in ensuring that children get the support that they need. SENDCOs work in a collaborative manner, **modelling** excellent practice in the classroom to class teachers who may ask how best to support a child, demonstrating ways in which our young people's learning can be made accessible, and also **auditing** teaching and learning in school to ensure that support is happening, and that it is meaningful.

SENDCOs make sure that our teaching of children with SEND is robust and rigorous, with **high expectations**, enabling those young people to fully access their curriculum and achieve their potential. The SENDCO puts plans in place for children following assessment, and then monitors those plans, the impact they are having, reviewing when necessary, and tweaking when needed. This cycle of '**assess, plan, do, review**', is not a linear process and instead will be circled back on – needs-led.

The SENDCO of a school is also the person who will have a vision of inclusion for children with SEND and what that will look like. This will feed into the headteacher's whole-school vision for inclusion. True inclusion should be about the entire staff, our parents and families, the governors, and the local community feeling and being included – being listened to, and feeling heard, with impactful actions taking place when necessary. It is something to which we can all contribute. To achieve this, and to make meaningful, measurable impact, SENDCOs have to **engage** and **inspire** those around them, motivating and activating them to move forwards in collaboration. It is a role that brings great rewards – but in schools that may have 1500+ children in them, it is also a big job.

Your SENDCO will most likely lead your Learning Support Department, or similar, and they will make you aware of procedures and processes. Know who your SENDCO is, show them some appreciation and demonstrate your support for children with SEND, and they will show the same appreciation for you. Members of staff who acknowledge SEND, who adapt their teaching and approaches, and who ask for and value support where needed, are proverbial music to the ears of SENDCOs. Go to your SENDCO not only with problems, although of course they are there to support with these, but go armed also with *solutions*. Even if you aren't sure how successful your ideas for strategies will be, just having taken the care and time to think of them shows your dedication.

So, go forth and find your SENDCO, don't leave them feeling lonely. Furthermore, form a mutual appreciation society with them and not only will you benefit, but the children and young people will too, and that's what it's all about.

Do you know who your **SENDCO** is?

How often do you seek advice from your SENDCO?

How many staff are there in your Learning Support Department? (In smaller schools, it may well be just the SENDCO and your support staff.)

Does your SENDCO teach in class as well, or are they non-teaching? (Do they have time to teach?!)

CHAPTER 2: WHAT ARE SEND?

Takeaways

- The **SEND Code of Practice** gives us statutory guidance around SEND support in schools. It tells us that we are '**all teachers of SEND**'.
- We should be mindful regarding the language that we use around needs and **take our lead** from our children with SEND and their families.
- There are **4 broad areas of need** – these are identified in the Code of Practice.
- To build truly inclusive classrooms, we should equip ourselves with knowledge around **neurodiversity**.

- We do not need to await a diagnosis for a child before we adapt our teaching for them – we should be **led by needs** and not by diagnosis.
- There may be particular **plans** for children with additional needs and our SENDCO will make us aware of them.
- Using a model of **cause and effect** helps us to remember to identify the cause (unmet needs) of the effects that we see in our classrooms, thereby effecting positive change.
- Our **SENDCO** co-ordinates SEND provision and is a key member of staff and point of call.

COMING UP NEXT

- **Chapter 3** is going to look at the **what** and the **why** of **relational approaches** – what they are, what they are not, and why we need to use them and build our inclusive classroom upon them.
- **Chapter 4** will then consider the **how** of **relational approaches** – detailing 4 pedagogies to use as the foundation on which your inclusive classroom will stand, including practical ideas and guidance.

Out of the Mouths of Staff

I've always believed that the Learning Support (LS) team are a vital and underappreciated part of an effective school. I believe classrooms benefit hugely from having a member of LS staff present, to not just support their 'allocated' pupil but to be another pair of hands to circulate and support individuals. In the wake of the pandemic there are more and more SEMH issues, so in some classes it's easy to feel you're fighting fires. I also think support from Emotional Literacy Support Assistants (ELSAs) is vital. I go out of my way to make these staff feel appreciated!

Teacher, Secondary

I find my SENDCO to be super supportive but run off their feet. There don't seem to be enough hours in the day anymore. I've been teaching for a long time and support for children with SEND has changed a lot over the years. It needed to – it's just a shame the funding hasn't changed with it.

Class Teacher, Primary

I find the best way to teach with *all* children is to make 'FUN' the key learning *within* the target. Teaching, whilst allowing the pupil to enjoy the task, is key. When teaching a child with SEND, I will explain the task in a variety of ways depending on the individual child's needs, but I find in my subject, PE, the best way is to *show* pupils how. I also think it's important for *all* pupils to understand what it is like to discover things for themselves. So, I will deliberately allow pupils to learn through play, this may lead to them 'failing' but it is important for them to do this in a positive way, as it will allow them to learn life skills in the process.

PE Teacher, Secondary

What I have learnt over the years is that one mould does not fit all. Even after 15 years of teaching, I still come across the students who surprise me with new challenges. When it comes to adapting my teaching for students with SEND, I try not to assume that a previously tried-and-tested strategy will fit. As a teacher, you have to learn how that student ticks, what works, what doesn't work, what their fears are and what really connects for them when it comes to learning. You have to get to know the individual before you decide what learning strategy is going to work. If I were to pick a common issue that I see for students with SEND, especially in a Performing Arts space (very open and no tables to hide behind) is confidence within their own ability. Lots of students with SEND have low confidence in themselves, so a key strategy I always start with is creating a positive "SAFE" environment and using praise and encouragement for even the tiniest little thing to help them feel safe and confident in my class.

Performing Arts Teacher, Secondary

Our SEND and Learning Support Department are very important to me! They hold a wealth of knowledge about our students and how to support them and meet their needs. For me, I have found that it is useful to be able to discuss concerns around a student and whether they may be due to an underlying SEND, and how to help these children with overcoming barriers.

In some instances, it might be that being in a whole-class setting with up to 29 other children is just too overwhelming for a child, and the SEND department and provisions mean that these children can still access a mainstream school, through an adapted and personalised curriculum.

History Teacher, Secondary

References

Autism Education Trust, Terminology Guide. Available at: https://www.autismeducationtrust.org.uk/sites/default/files/2021-09/terminology_guide.pdf

National Autistic Society. Available at: https://www.autism.org.uk/what-we-do/help-and-support/how-to-talk-about-autism (Accessed: 16 July 2023)

Neurodiversityhub. Available at: https://www.neurodiversityhub.org/what-is-neurodiversity

The SEND Code of Practice: Ref: DFE-00205-2013. Department for Education and Department of Health. (2015). *Special Educational Needs and Disability Code of Practice: 0 to 25 Years.* Available at: https://www.gov.uk/government/publications/send-code-of-practice-0-to-25 (Accessed: 10 July 2023). *The 4 Broad Areas of Need can be found on pages 97–98.

Chapter Three

The What and The Why of Relational Approaches

In this chapter, we are going to look at the **what** and the **why** of relational approaches, because they will provide the solid foundation for your inclusive classroom.

The chapter is therefore in 2 parts.

Part 1: This will explain **what** relational approaches *are*, and what they *are not* – including how supportive they are for all children, but especially those with SEND.

Part 2: This will explore **why** relational approaches matter so much and **why** we need to use them, by putting them into context via exploring the needs of children and young people in 21st-century classrooms.

When we move on to Chapter 4, we'll look at **how** to use them.

Part 1 The What	Summary
Your Toolkit	A recap of our **Toolkit** model with which to build our inclusive classrooms, and a recap of our model of **Cause and Effect** to help us identify and support needs.
Relationships and Relational Approaches	What they are and are not. In short, they're not a soft touch, and they lead to long-term success and last a lifetime.
Unconditional Positive Regard	What do we mean by this? What role does it play in relational approaches?
Part 2 The Why	Summary
Trust and Maslow's Hierarchy of Needs	We will examine **Maslow's Hierarchy** and then an in-school equivalent of it to gain some context regarding the children in our classrooms – where they are coming from, plus what they are coming to us with.
Social, Emotional and Mental Health (SEMH) and the Reality of Behaviour	A look at the statistics behind exclusion, the prevalence of **SEMH** needs, and the reality of how tough it can be to support some behaviours. We will also delve into '**I just want to teach**' and what 'teaching' actually is these days, progressing to discuss the '**ejector seat**' policies that some schools incorporate and the detriment of removing children from our classrooms.
What About Relationships Outside of School?	Screentime, devices, lockdowns, pandemics, and social interaction: how these exacerbated SEMH needs.

DOI: 10.4324/b23417-4

Adverse Childhood Experiences (ACEs) **Trauma Recovery** **Attachment Disorders**	We will look at how ACEs, accompanying trauma, and any resulting attachment disorders, may present. We'll also consider how we, as teachers, can provide some reparation for children who have experienced or present with these, being their readily **available trusted adults**. Our prior discussions around **Maslow, trust, SEMH and Unconditional Positive Regard (UPR)**, will come together here.

Part 1

The 'What' of Relational Approaches

There are 2 models that we looked at in Chapters 1 and 2 that will be referred to throughout this book. These are:

- The blueprint for your **Toolkit** to build your inclusive classroom; and
- Our model of **Cause and Effect**.

We need to be mindful of both to meet needs in our classrooms and to solidify our relational foundation, so let's both recap and expand upon them.

Your Toolkit

In Chapters 1 and 2, we established our core understanding of SEND and of how adaptive teaching is excellent teaching for all. Now, in Chapter 3, we can move on to examine how we can build our inclusive classroom. The blueprint for this is as shown in Figure 3.1.

Within the large community of the school, your classroom is, in effect, your home. It is a subcommunity and the children within it will flourish best when it is inclusive. Yes, there are policies in place and expectations that differ from school to school, but your classroom is one that you can build from the relational ground up. Traditionally, we think of old-style differentiation as referring to making different resources and so forth for different sets of children, with less focus on differentiating our approaches for children. Adaptive teaching lends itself more readily to adapting our approaches as opposed to just the work that goes on in the classroom.

The metaphor of the classroom as a home is nothing new,[1] and nor is the term 'scaffolding' as referring to a temporary support, but underneath everything else, underpinning learning within your classroom before that learning can even begin, are the **relationships**. This includes yours with the children and other adults in the room, and also the relationships between the children themselves. The key to this is consistency; consistency of approach, of expectation, and of behaviour. It involves your **knowing the children**, as we discussed in the previous chapter, and also the **children knowing *you***.

---

1 Examples include Rachel Cosgrove's model in her book (2020), *Inclusive Teaching in a Nutshell: A Visual Guide for Busy Teachers*. England, Routledge Publishing.

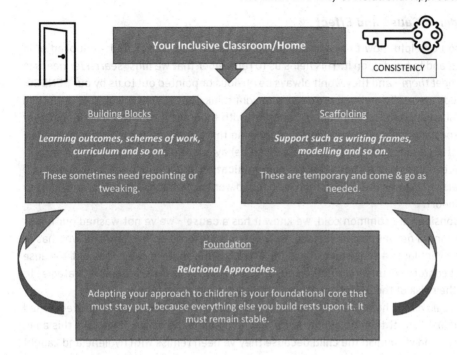

Figure 3.1 Your inclusive classroom/home model

By remaining consistent, our young people know what to expect; it sets a clear boundary for them. It's also easier said than done, especially when we are tired, but if we let things slip and allow Phoebe to look at her phone quickly under the table, or allow Zaid to call out answers despite having a 'hands up' expectation, then every other beady-eyed child in that room will soon cotton onto it, and we only make life harder for ourselves. So, consistency opens the door of the classroom, it lets us in, and our relational approaches provide a solid foundation for our room to stand upon. We do not want to be on shaky, inconsistent ground and, even though they may not realise it, nor do the children.

We've all been there. Think of a time when you've seen a child doing something they shouldn't in class and you've let it slide. Was it low-level disruption? A sly snoop at a phone under the desk?

Sometimes ignoring is tactical, sometimes it's doomful. When it's the latter, we know we should have picked up on it. Otherwise, it can become very hard, once we've been inconsistent, to rein things back in.

This consistency also applies to our relationships in our classrooms. No matter our own personal mood, we must maintain consistency to show ourselves to be a trustworthy adult.

Our Model of Cause and Effect

It will also be helpful now to revisit our model of **Cause and Effect** that we looked at in Chapter 2, and to build upon it. This helps us to remember that we must *search for needs* in order to *meet them* – and they won't always be obvious or pointed out to us by our SENDCO. Some needs are easily met and are what we might think of as more typical, such as a child with visual impairment sitting nearer the board with thoughtful classroom lighting. Other needs, especially those around SEMH, are the kind that we will hear some teachers referring to not as 'needs' at all but, instead, as 'bad behaviour'. Relational approaches encourage us to recognise that **all behaviour is communication**; it's trying to tell us something. If we ever wish to change the **effect**, then we need to work out what the **cause** is, and address it with support.

If we consider the common cold, we know it has a **cause** – we've not washed our hands after touching a germ-infested surface, we've been spluttered on by someone who has it, we haven't ventilated a space and so on. The **effect** then is that we catch the cold. Because in the 21st century we understand the **cause**, we can teach our own kids some strategies to mitigate their risk of the **effect**, and these strategies will be helpful.

What would *not* be helpful at all, is for us to never teach our children these strategies and to instead just expect them to simply know how to manage the cause. If we take this analogy further, and we punish the child because they've been remiss with hygiene and caught the cold – and if we expect this punishment to mean that they won't catch one again even though we *still* don't teach them the strategies of how to avoid doing so – then is that child any better placed to remain healthy? Are we going to avoid the effect (the cold) if we never teach the young person how to manage the cause (germs)? Of course not. For embedded, long-term effects, it's always better to be preventative when it comes to the root cause. And this is why **relational approaches** are so important (Figure 3.2).

Relationships and Relational Approaches

What Relational Approaches Are and What Relational Approaches Are Not

First up, relational approaches are not about being mates with the students, or bending boundaries, or being pushovers. Quite the opposite.

Secondly, in 1938, Harvard University began what has since transpired to be one of the longest running studies into Adult Development in the world, which is still continuing now. Some of the initial recruits included John F. Kennedy, and since the study first began, the children of those initial recruits have also been included, as have varying other groups. Interestingly, there were no women in the first cohort because Harvard didn't admit women in those days; another way in which the world, and therefore teaching, has changed. The key finding from this study is that no matter what wealth has been accrued, or what career paths people have chosen to follow, the central factor that truly makes the difference to both **emotional happiness** and **physical health** is the fostering of happy, healthy relationships. More than money, fame, IQ, or genetics, *happy relationships are the foundation and*

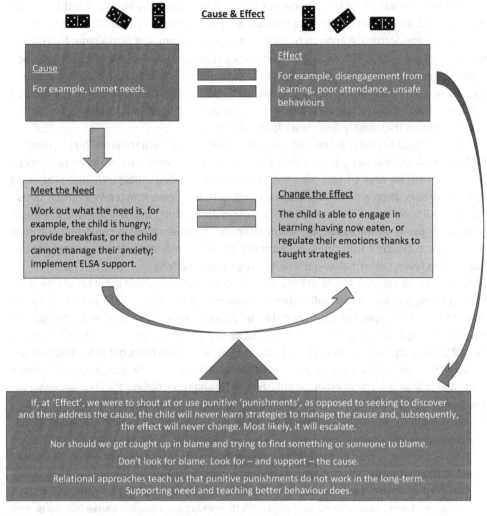

Cause & Effect

Cause

For example, unmet needs.

=

Effect

For example, disengagement from learning, poor attendance, unsafe behaviours

Meet the Need

Work out what the need is, for example, the child is hungry; provide breakfast, or the child cannot manage their anxiety; implement ELSA support.

=

Change the Effect

The child is able to engage in learning having now eaten, or regulate their emotions thanks to taught strategies.

If, at 'Effect', we were to shout at or use punitive 'punishments', as opposed to seeking to discover and then address the cause, the child will never learn strategies to manage the cause and, subsequently, the effect will never change. Most likely, it will escalate.

Nor should we get caught up in blame and trying to find something or someone to blame.

Don't look for blame. Look for – and support – the cause.

Relational approaches teach us that punitive punishments do not work in the long-term. Supporting need and teaching better behaviour does.

Figure 3.2 Taking our model of Cause and Effect a little further

core of life (The Harvard Gazette 2017). It makes perfect sense then that they are also the foundation of your inclusive classroom.

How have relationships, both personal and professional, made a **difference** in your life?

Can you think of one relationship - whether at home or school - that has provided consistent, **unconditional** support for you? Who is it with? Why is it more supportive than others?

Are there any relationships that you know could be improved? Have you taken steps to improve them? If not, why? What has stopped you?

Over the past decade or so, the schools in which I have worked, the local authority in which I have worked, and the fact that I have specialised within inclusion and SEND, have all meant that I have been fortunate enough to receive a significant amount of training, from some inspirational people, about explicit relational approaches. I have seen schools in which there is a fantastic atmosphere between staff and children and where all stakeholders have been trained in relational practice, but I have also seen schools that have instead developed an 'us and them' culture, almost a power struggle between staff and children, with purely punitive policies that simply don't work in the long-term.

It goes without saying that the staff in a school need to be **authoritative**, just as parents do. Relational approaches are not about being a soft touch where we are seen to be weak and ineffective; we aren't being mates with the kids or smiling indulgently and proffering a custard cream when a 5-year-old tells us to f*** off. But being firm (or even strict, to use a more traditional term) does not mean shouting and losing control. Firm doesn't mean belittling or being an **unresponsive** *authoritarian*. Firm means being consistent with our approaches, consistent with **rules** and **boundaries**, and consistent with our **consequences** (that should teach better behaviour). Firm is **high expectations**.

Sometimes we may need to adjust or adapt our consequences or our expectations because we must be responsive – a child with Tourette Syndrome cannot be expected to sit in silence in an assembly for example, but nor should they be excluded from it, nor receive a consequence if they tic during it, and they should certainly not be 'punished' for doing so. All teachers worth their QTS would agree with this because that child has an obvious need, but some teachers will still agree that, for certain children and young people, it's OK to use language such as 'punishment', and to also implement practical punishment or what they believe the children 'deserve'. However, if we are thinking from a relational perspective, then punishing children (which, let's be frank, used to involve hitting them) is not going to solve the *cause* of the behaviour. Consequences = yes; punishment = no. We all need to learn that there are consequences for our behaviours, but they should be **thoughtful consequences** that get to the root of the cause, they should not be based on how to best retaliate with punitive measures. Relational approaches are not about us all being a 'bunch of Leftie snowflakes' who try to buddy up with the kids, but they are about taking a more intelligent approach to working out what the **cause** (e.g. an unmet need) is of the **effect** (e.g. behaviour), and then putting in place strategies to support it, and ultimately teaching our young people strategies to support themselves.

Can you think of a student who is repeatedly 'punished' in school with puni- tive consequences that have no long-term positive effect, catching them in a cycle of 'poor behaviour – punishment – poor behaviour – punishment'?

What are those punitive consequences?

What meaningful consequences could be used instead to support that student in learning better behaviours, and valuing them?

 How could those consequences be planned to support the **cause** (unmet need) of the **effect** (the behaviour)?

The schools that I have been in where students respect the staff the most have always been the schools where relational approaches were followed explicitly, being written into policy and incorporated in training for all staff regarding why relational approaches are needed (and we'll be moving on to this shortly) and how to employ the techniques (which we shall look at in Chapter 4).

It needs to be emphasised, however, that we can have all the training in the world but if we are not then mindful of that training, seeking to employ it consistently in all that we do, then the training is wasted. It's all down to our willingness to learn new things and, sometimes, to unlearn our prior practice. Of course, if you are a class teacher reading this, then you have little control over school policy, but what you do have control over is your classroom and the foundations that you want to build it upon. In Chapter 4, we will look at **4 core relational approaches** or pedagogies that you can use and dip in to, so that you can achieve exactly that.

'I Am Relational, I Always Ask the Kids How They Are'

The vast majority of teachers, by the very nature of the job, will be relational to some extent, but *explicit* relational approaches go deeper than a surface level and instead drill into the real bedrock. We are back to that mindfulness again; keeping at the fore of our minds how we are talking to children and young people, what our body language says, what our tone says. Just saying 'good morning' to the children is not an explicit relational approach. It's a great start and it's modelling of basic manners, but relational approaches go much further than this and, if we manage to, we can have excellent success with young people and achieve outcomes that are brilliant for them.

We need to bear in mind that excellent outcomes do not look the same for everyone. We need to be aspirational for children and young people and we need to encourage their own aspirations, but we must also acknowledge that not every child is going to be university-ready, and nor should they be. However, they should be future-ready by the time they leave us – whether they are leaving us to transition to Year 1, or to the next key stage, or they are leaving us at 16. The key responsibility of our job is to make sure children are ready; ready for the short-term future and ready for the long-term future. And healthy relationships will give them the best start at this.

Can you think of one child you have taught who has left you **'future-ready'**, whether to transition to a new year group or school, or to leave school in Year 11?

How did you know they were future-ready?

How can we **personalise** what 'future-ready' means for each child?

When I worked in a school that was an Alternative Provision (AP), that was attended by children who had been excluded from mainstream, relationships were at the crux of everything we did. We were working with some of the most challenging and highly vulnerable children in the city and, subsequently, we had to adapt our approaches before we could even begin to academically teach. Whilst building those relationships we were, by proxy, modelling them, whilst teaching the importance of Social and Emotional Aspects of Learning, or SEAL, just by engaging youngsters in conversations and showing an authentic interest in them; listening to them, valuing what they were telling us about their life experiences or their interests.

Some of the children we would teach were no longer in mainstream due to health reasons, whether physical health or mental health, and the young people would present with a plethora of needs. Parents or carers were closely involved, and subsequently the entire process was significantly more inclusive than mainstream is logistically able to be. For example, reintegration was a specialism and we could find ourselves teaching in the home of a child from behind a closed bedroom door initially (with no clue as to whether or not we were actually just talking to the family cat). This would incorporate a lot of babbling, feigning that you were perfectly comfortable with the situation yourself (fake it 'til you make it, if you will), and striving to show the young person – who you hadn't even clapped eyes on yet – that you were kind enough, approachable enough, and trustworthy enough, for them to eventually show their face on the other side of that door. That key of consistency pays off; it opens the door for us.

Unconditional Positive Regard

Finally in Part One, we must consider Unconditional Positive Regard (UPR), because this will play into each of the 4 core relational approaches that we will look at in Chapter 4.

UPR was initially developed by **Carl Rogers**, an American psychologist, who was also known for his person-centred approaches (inclusion bells may ring). According to Rogers, UPR means that we fully accept a person, with **no conditions** placed upon our warmth towards them and our genuine care (Cherry 2020). If children receive this from their families during their early years and beyond, then it makes sense that their self-worth and self-esteem will thus be nurtured and, in turn, develop. However, as we know, plenty of children for myriad reasons are not necessarily raised with UPR. As we shall see when we move on to Part 2 of this chapter, we bear witness in school to the detriments of this each and every day. Some children are not treated with UPR at school either – but they absolutely should be.

What we should ensure as teachers, is that we *always* employ unconditional positive regard when supporting young people. And this includes when they flip a chair and tell you their suspicions about your mother and what they think she gets up to in private. It is worth reiterating that, as with all relational approaches, this does **not mean** that we are being weak or condoning this kind of behaviour. We must employ that key of consistency with meaningful consequences. We are in charge of our classrooms. We must teach better behaviour and show why it's to be valued, but we should avoid retaliation. We should avoid losing control and shouting. The latter only makes us feel better, in the short-term, and does nothing for the child. Nor will it lead to better outcomes.

It is crucial that we do not get sucked into **retaliatory banter** with children and young people. The temptation is there and, given that we are adults, we can no doubt pick holes in their arguments and escalate the situation – but is this what we should be modelling? Is this the behaviour we should be teaching? Will it encourage respect? No, no, and no.

Philippa Perry, a British psychotherapist, speaks about how parents get drawn into **'Fact Tennis'** with their kids; essentially competing in unproductive, point-scoring arguments (Perry 2019). Whether you are a parent or a teacher, you will recognise this. With our barely realising it at the time, we get hooked into point-for-point scoring. We know that this achieves nothing and, instead, we need to move forwards and do so with UPR. Getting involved in tit-for-tat arguments doesn't move us forward in finding solutions, it only escalates problems or distracts entirely from the issue at hand. We get trapped in the **effect**, and we forget to discover and support the initial **cause**.

Whilst we are considering UPR and, in terms of kindness and relational behaviour policies, should you be in a position to write or contribute to such a policy, then the work of **Dave Whitaker** might be right up your inclusive street (Whitaker 2021). Whitaker propounds that kindness should be at the heart of all we do with children (and who can argue with that?) He also details a no-exclusion policy that he embedded in his school when he was a headteacher, which makes for inspiring reading if you are in a position to elicit change at a whole-school strategic level, and are prepared to embrace inclusion at the core of all that you do.

Can you think now of a time when you have engaged in Fact Tennis with a child? Or been sucked into **retaliatory banter**? What happened? Did it support the child or just make you feel better?

Are there children whom you **do not** treat with UPR? It can be uncomfortable to admit even in our own heads, but are there children you dislike in school? How do you treat them? How could you treat them to make a difference?

Can you identify a specific child/children whom you could now begin treating with UPR – consistently, from here on in – reminding yourself when it gets tough why you should do so?

PART 1: THE 'WHAT' OF RELATIONAL APPROACHES

Takeaways

- **Consistency** is key.
- We must search for the **causes** (needs) of the **effects** that we see in our classrooms and support them.
- Relationships are the **most important** – and can be the most beneficial – things in our lives.
- The success of our classrooms depends upon the success of the relationships within them.
- Relational approaches embed **long-term effects** as opposed to being superficial sticking plasters.
- Relational approaches are **never** a 'soft touch'. They are about **high expectations**.

- Punitive punishments do not work in the long-term; **meaningful consequences** do.
- We must **build connections** with children and to do this, children must trust us.
- We should always, **no matter what**, treat children with UPR. This does not mean condoning poor behaviour.

Part 2

The 'Why' of Relational Approaches

In Part 2, let's explore **why** relational approaches matter so much and **why** we need to use them, by putting them into context via exploring the needs of children and young people in 21st-century classrooms.

This section will include:

Part 2 The Why	Summary
Trust and Maslow's Hierarchy of Needs	We will examine **Maslow's Hierarchy** and then an in-school equivalent of it to gain some context regarding the children in our classrooms – where they are coming from, plus what they are coming to us with.
Social, Emotional, and Mental Health (SEMH) and Behaviour	A look at the statistics behind exclusion, the prevalence of **SEMH** needs, and the reality of how tough it can be to support some behaviours. We will also delve into '**I just want to teach**' and what 'teaching' actually is these days, progressing to discuss the '**ejector seat**' policies that some schools incorporate and the detriment of removing children from our classrooms.
What About Relationships Outside of School?	Screentime, devices, lockdowns, pandemics, and social interaction: how these exacerbated SEMH needs.
Adverse Childhood Experiences (ACEs) Trauma Recovery Attachment Disorders	We will look at how ACEs, accompanying trauma, and any resulting attachment disorders, may present. We'll also consider how we, as teachers, can provide some reparation for children who have experienced or present with these, being their **readily available trusted adults**. Our prior discussions around **Maslow, trust, SEMH and UPR**, will come together here.

Trust and Maslow's Hierarchy of Needs

Stop for a moment and consider how many people in your life do you **trust implicitly**? There is every chance that the total count is very few.

How many people in **school** do you trust *implicitly*? Anyone?

How many members of your family? Perhaps you trust some people with certain things – such as access to your bank account, shared maybe with a partner – and not with others?

Trusting people is a thorny issue. In a 21st-century world of instant news stories, or social media, perhaps it's even harder. Much of our ability to trust rests upon our past experiences or our childhoods. Remember back in Chapter 1 when I told you a little of mine; if you think of your own, you may be able to identify experiences that directly correlate to the relationships that you now have as an adult. Everything has a **cause and an effect**, and that's no different for the children that we teach. The difference for us is that we are adults now, but when we're kids, we have far less control over what goes on around us and what choices we are able to make, or, conversely, what things are chosen for us. This concept of choice is important and links also to Chapter 2, when we considered how children with SEND, or parents of those children, can seek some empowerment by exercising their control over how their needs are spoken about and referred to. Choice gives us some control, when we may otherwise feel as though we have little to none.

If we consider that our day jobs involve welcoming between 30 and several hundred children and young people into our classrooms, then we have to acknowledge that not all of those children and young people are actually going to arrive trusting us. Our education system is to all intents and purposes built upon the premise that youngsters come to school ready to trust teachers and ready to learn. I don't know what that looked like 80 years ago (although given that canes were used as a method of control, I am willing to guess), but these days it just isn't so: not all young people come into the school building ready to learn and ready to trust. There are myriad reasons for this, some of which are heartbreaking, many of which are deeply complex, some of which might be linked to specific needs.

You may well have heard of **Maslow's Hierarchy of Needs**. It is called a hierarchy because it's based on the idea that all humans have particular needs, beginning with the absolute basics (such as air, which I think we can all agree is a necessity), and progressing steadily upwards to the desire to 'become the most that one can be'; in other words, to fulfil our potential. If we consider the students coming into our schools then, can we say that some of their **most basic needs** have definitely been met before they walk through the gates? Some of those other basic needs include shelter, warmth, and clothing. When we consider the cost of living or the areas of deprivation that some of us teach in, can we really say that all students have access to the most basic needs a human should be in receipt of? Absolutely not.

Below is a summary of Maslow's Hierarchy with an in-school equivalent. As you'll see, until Step 1 is met, the child cannot progress to Step 2 and so forth. At which step do you believe the child is ready to learn? I've suggested Step 4 but your opinion may differ according to your experiences.

Summary of Maslow's 5 Needs	In-School Equivalent (Consider cause and effect – can we support the root cause to help us mitigate the effect?)
5 Self-Actualisation Morality, creativity, achieving full potential.	The child engages in learning and is able to fulfil their own personal potential. Be future-ready. Inspire them to aspire. Dare them to dream.
4 Esteem Confidence, respect, self-esteem, achievement.	Encourage, use careful and meaningful praise, use appropriate rewards, recognise achievement, involve families with this where appropriate. Model respect and also self-respect. Avoid carrot-on-stick rewards to tempt the child to complete work or behave in a particular manner, instead teach better behaviour and teach why it's better. **The child is ready to learn.**
3 Love/Belonging Friendships, family, romantic relationships.	Once the child begins to trust you and you know them better, you can be more playful (never sarcastic). Teach through play, adapt teaching through play (see Chapter 4). This can be for teenagers as well as younger children. Use humour, laugh together with the child. Value the child's voice and opinions, show them you've listened and heard them. Help them to feel that they belong and that they are accepted and valued for who they are. This is inclusion. Encourage friendships. The child is **becoming** ready and open to learning now.
2 Safety Security of body, family, health, employment.	Build a relationship with the child, make your classroom a safe space. Take time to chat with the young people. Ask after their interests, remember things they tell you and then refer to them at later chosen moments. Remain calm but consistent. Use non-verbal empathy, mindful of body language. Adapt your *approach* as well as your lessons. Build trust and don't judge the child. Make the child feel safe in your consistent classroom with your solid relational foundation. Accept who the child is and where they've come from but maintain high expectations. Use high challenge and high support. Employ unconditional positive regard. Refer to DSL and external agency support where needed. The child is unlikely to be ready to learn if these needs are not yet met.
1 Physiological Air, food, water and so on.	Recognise that the child may not have eaten at home, or feel loved, or have a safe bed for the night. They may not have basic needs met – find out about them, be curious, meet the needs that aren't met – look at the cause of the need not being met too. Consider whether school provide a uniform? Does school provide breakfast? Can leftover canteen food be saved and distributed after lunch to children who may need it? They may be highly resistant at first – possibly for months/years – do not desist. Be persistent and consistent. How can external agencies support? Do you need to refer to Designated Safeguarding Lead (DSL)? The child is unlikely to be ready to learn.

Each step must be met before we can move to the next

Consistency is key throughout

Within this model, we can see that until one of Maslow's steps is firmly in place, we cannot progress to the next, and we may even go up and down. We need to have those basic needs met consistently before we are ready to move on. We can't achieve our full potential if we haven't eaten properly for days and have nowhere safe to sleep. In school, we can support the child but we also need to accept that this can take a long time. If you think back to those examples of who you either do or do not trust in life, how long did it take for you to trust some of those people or that person? It won't have been instant, it may have taken **years**.

We have to accept then, that just as it takes us years as adults to have faith in someone, so it does for some young people. Just because we are teachers, doesn't mean people trust us. Depending on their own school experiences, it might in fact mean quite the opposite! Even when we meet with parents sometimes this is clear; they will tell us of their own school experiences and what those looked like, and how these have affected their opinions towards us. Again then, we see how **building relationships is key to building inclusion**.

Are your own basic needs being met at the moment? And if they are not, then do you know how and where to seek support? It's just as crucial that our needs as met as those of our students. We spoke in Chapter 1 about our own oxygen masks – always seek support when you need it.

Are there students who you know are not having their basic needs met at the moment? How are the school supporting with this? How might the **cause and effect** model help you to do so?

SEMH and Behaviour

What is behaviour like in your current school?

Do you notice any **patterns** to behaviour?

Does your school have a '**Relational Policy**' or a '**Behaviour Policy**'? (Or both?)

Are there any students whose behaviour you struggle with, or who you dread teaching because of behaviour? Can you find a **cause** for the **effects**?

Relational approaches, as with excellent adaptive teaching, are excellent for all children, with or without SEND, but they are particularly helpful for children who have SEMH needs. You will remember from Chapter 2 that SEMH is one of the 4 broad areas of SEND, and sub-sequently one of those that an EHCP can be written for and provide support in.

The chances are that SEMH needs in your school have risen in line with national statistics for SEMH. This is now the second most prevalent SEND in schools (Special Educational Needs in England 2023), rising as children progress through into secondary education (and perhaps also being recognised and identified more in secondary schools). If we look back to the SEND Code of Practice and the descriptors of areas of need that we examined in Chapter 2, SEMH is described as:

6.32 – Children and young people may experience a wide range of social and emotional difficulties which manifest themselves in many ways. These may include becoming with-drawn or isolated, as well as displaying challenging, disruptive or disturbing behaviour. These behaviours may signify underlying mental health difficulties such as anxiety or depression, self-harming, substance misuse, eating disorders or physical symptoms that are medically unexplained. Other children and young people may have disorders such as attention deficit disorder, attention deficit hyperactive disorder or attachment disorder.

It is worth noting then that, statistically, **47% of exclusions are of children with SEND** and, furthermore, that 60% of those exclusions are children whose area of need is identified as being SEMH (SEND Network 2023). You yourself may have identified a significant rise in your own school and we'll move on later in this chapter to consider how the pandemic and the use of mobile phones have not been helpful, but this is a more complex issue than those factors alone. Your SENDCO, SLT, family link workers and so on (including yourself) will be putting support in place outside of the classroom for these children, but we need to look at what more you can be doing inside the classroom, and relational approaches will be a key part of this.

As the Code of Practice states, SEMH may well show itself as a need via behaviours in school. Let's make no bones about it: this is truly testing as a teacher. No doubt you've planned some terrific lessons in the past, only to have them effectively blown apart by the behaviour of a minority of children. You may have said, or heard others saying, '**I just want to teach!**' You may have heard, or said yourself, '**Why are these children still here?!**' Ditto for, '**These kids are feral!**' and '**I blame the parents!**' There's no getting away from it, these are phrases we will have all heard and that some of us will have used, so let's be transparent about it because, after all, the very reason that I have written this book – and the very reason you're reading it – is because we want to effect positive change for children. Nobody goes into teaching if they don't like kids (if they do, more fool them, surely they don't stay in it for long?!). Instead, we go into it to make life better for children, to instil our passion in them, to make the community we live in a better place, and to get job satisfaction through doing so. However, it's extremely tough. You may well get hurt in a classroom – again, let's be transparent, anything less is both patronising and evokes a false narrative. You may be scared in a classroom. Absolutely none of this is OK. But, much as it's not OK, is it, sadly, a reality. But it is a reality we can **change**.

'I Just Want to Teach!'

Is this something you have said yourself? (I imagine plenty of us have, if we are honest.)

What does 'teaching' mean to you?

When we say, 'I just want to teach', then we must be accepting of the fact that said 'teaching' does entail behaviour management and this can be challenging. Your school, hopefully, is supportive. Fingers crossed, if you're experiencing this, then your SLT are on it and your line manager, or pals in the staffroom, are there for you. Systems should be in place for that child to have meaningful consequences that teach better behaviour, for support around the child's needs, or mental health, or around their family, and around meeting those needs that Maslow identified. Your school is hopefully looking at what that behaviour is trying to communicate, and what needs are, as yet, unmet. But, of course, your own needs have to be met, too.

As professional adults, we are at least in a better place to meet those needs for ourselves than children are for themselves – think back to Chapter 1 and knowing your support networks and setting your own boundaries. But think also of the child who does not have a safe space to sleep at night. Or whose home has 2 bedrooms, 6 siblings, and no carpets or clean bedding. Try also to not take anything personally, however impossible this may seem. Words like 'feral' are easily thrown around about children but if we were watching the life stories of some of the young people whom we teach being played out in a documentary, as opposed to in our classrooms, we'd be filled with empathy. We'd understand how that might exhibit in behaviours. Of course, it's tougher when it's happening to us but, no matter how hard, we need to try and resist blame, resist referring to children in derogatory terms, and resist believing that teaching in the 21st century = delivering lessons to a set of 30 'model' students.

We should have high expectations of our teaching, but we must be realistic too, otherwise we risk being in for a hell of a fall. When we say we 'just want to teach', we need to be honest about what teaching is. It is not the same as the teaching of the 1950s, because umpteen decades have passed since then. **The world has changed, and teaching with it**. This links us back to the language that we use around young people, which is something we've focused on throughout the book so far, because it is so important. Yes, we need to vent to others, but at appropriate moments in appropriate places. We need to get it out of our system, firmly reminding ourselves that each day is another chance. We evaporate our recriminations at home, we return, and we ensure that we are ready to go again with new strategies and adaptive approaches. **We can do this**.

'Why Are These Kids Still Here?!' – Inclusion, Exclusion and The Ejector Seat

In response to 'Why are these kids still here?!', the reason for that is – as you may have guessed – **inclusion**. You most likely know that exclusion does not work. A child is excluded for the day; back they bounce the following, behaving in no different a manner than that which landed them with their day/s off to start with.

Perhaps your school has a system whereby the young people have a '**3 strikes and you're out**' policy, for example. On the third strike, the child is removed from the class and sent to some form of internal exclusion room. But does the child then return to the next lesson, behaving perfectly and demonstrating respect for you? Most likely not. In fact, having a system whereby children are removed from learning rather leaves the door open to inadvertently training both staff and children alike that the latter do not have to be in a classroom. What this kind of policy definitely does not do is encourage teachers to work *harder* at building relationships and adapting their teaching in order to really support the young people and engage them. Because of this, there are some schools which make their expectations clear that your students stay in learning (as long as they do not pose a danger), for example, being removed but placed in another lesson for that period. Alternatively, others may need short-term removal to an Additional Provision that is run with rigour, where specialist staff teach better behaviours and support needs, helping to remove barriers to learning, with the high expectation of reintegration to the mainstream, or whatever 'success' looks like for the individual so that their needs are met.

It's perfectly normal to go home at night as a teacher dwelling on some in-class horror that's occurred during the day, and then spend your evening sweating to think of how you can get it right the next day, or the next lesson. But sometimes, you'll find yourself not needing to practise managing behaviour purely because of the behaviour systems of the school in which you work, and this would be a tragedy. After all, if we train ourselves and the children to believe that if they aren't behaving then we can just get rid of them, then who wouldn't take that easy option? It's human nature. A little like having an **ejector seat** in the cockpit of the classroom.

If things go wrong in a lesson, ask yourself what can you do next time? There's always a chance to start again.

Can you identify the **cause** of why things went wrong, to positively change the **effect**?

What **resources** might you use or change?

What **adaptations** might you make?

What **external support** can you seek?

Policies that Remove Children from Learning

Policies that involve the removal of children from learning probably worked in some schools when they were initially introduced and when the previous expectation had correctly been that children stayed in your classroom with you. The shame of suddenly being removed from a lesson by a walkie-talkie sporting member of staff, getting transported to a miserable exclusion room and receiving a detention plus a call to their mortified parent may well have shocked some students into compliance. However, compliance – if we think back to our **cause and effect model** – does not equal meeting the needs of the root cause, and so it is but a **reactive sticking plaster**, whereas we need to think long-term.

Such ejector policies may also have raised staff morale initially because suddenly staff could 'just teach' without worrying about behaviour. But once this novelty wears off, and once staff start using the ejector seat more often for smaller, low-level misdemeanours, as opposed to only during emergency behavioural situations, then we begin to embed a culture and ethos of both children and teachers believing that the former do not have to remain in lessons with the latter. Ironically, the staff morale that was so much higher initially, because it was based on the misapprehension that behaviour was better in the school (as opposed to still continuing but just hidden in a room far, far away), will eventually plummet to new lows once the removed children – who now believe they don't need to be in classrooms – decide, rather logically, that they don't need to be in the exclusion rooms either. They may take instead to drifting around corridors at will, occasionally paying a visit to the lessons they used to attend, but probably just flipping staff the bird through the window or, worse still, barging into the room and creating as much havoc as they are able. Because after all, they've got no respect for the teacher who repeatedly turfed them out. Why would they? When a walkie-talkie sporter removes a child, they aren't going to then wave a wand and return that child, behaving impeccably, to the teacher who ejected them. In fact, because the child will have lost even more learning during their absence, if they didn't have gaps in knowledge and understanding before, they certainly will do now - and that in itself is not a recipe for success.

This wish for a **quick behaviour fix** via the ejector seat is understandable - similar to parents who hand a crying baby a phone because it makes life easier in the short-term but, in the long-term, it creates a rod for our own backs. Parents lose parenting and interaction skills - so do the babies. Teachers lose behaviour management skills - and then they lose the children. The danger we then face, is developing students who become persistent corridor wanderers, teachers who never practise and therefore never hone their behaviour management skills or adaptive teaching, and are subsequently left unable to deal with even low-level issues. Eventually, we see poor relationships with little mutual respect all round. Yes, the ejector seat means that the other children in the lesson, both with and without SEND, have a better learning experience whilst those who have been removed are absent, but this is not the ideal. The ideal is that young people stay in learning. **The ideal is that we are inclusive**. It is what we strive for.

What we do not achieve by using the ejector seat, is the teaching of better behaviour, or the encouragement of wanting to learn, or of how and why to make better choices. Detentions that are restorative - so those where the teacher who issued the DT goes to meet the child during the DT - are a wonderful idea, but are they always impactful? Not if they aren't managed meaningfully, with follow-ups from the class teacher in-between learning, where relationships are built and embedded.

Is there a **detention system** in your school?

Are there after-school DTs, lunch and break ones, or both?

Who **staffs** the DTs?

Is there a **restorative** element to them whereby the staff member who set the DT goes along to rebuild and maintain a positive relationship with the child?

Do the **same** children keep getting DTs?

Is the system successful - and what does '**successful**' look like?

Would It Work as a Parent?

If we imagine that we are parents (and perhaps you are), and we consider our young child speaking rudely to us or telling us to 'shut up', then hopefully we'd have a support strategy to calmly teach our child why that particular behaviour was not OK, and to look at what led to it – the cause – and how we can make it better. We would do this ourselves, because we care about our relationship with our child, and we would remind them when necessary of our expectations, modelling how we should speak to one another. We would do this firmly, consistently, but with kindness and respect.

What we would *not* do, is get someone else to come along, remove our child from our home for a few hours or days, and then expect that person to 'fix' that behaviour and return them to us, treating us with respect and never misbehaving again (much as we might want them to – for an easy life). It might work in the short term, out of shock, but it won't work in the long term. In fact, our child will lose respect for us because they can see we are unable to support them ourselves and nor do we **care** enough to invest in doing so. For our child to respect us, we must respect them, and the starting point for this is through our parent/child relationship. It is no different with our teacher/student relationships.

Another adult cannot foster it for you; it needs to start with you.

What About Relationships Outside of School?

Screentime, Lockdowns and Social Interaction

Whilst we look at behaviour and SEMH, it's worth discussing screens and lockdowns. There is no doubt that you and your colleagues engage in talk about this quite frequently! Statistically, we know that children returning to school after lockdowns, especially in primary schools, demonstrated poorer behaviour and corresponding difficulties with their mental health (Blanden et al. 2021). Anybody who taught before 2020, and who has taught since, has likely already identified how the pandemic adversely affected children – their mental health, their social skills, their transitions, and their behaviour – without reading this research. The stresses of the pandemic affected us all, and teaching since the pandemic is different to teaching before it.

Obviously teaching has to change and in many cases, rightly so; we must adapt endlessly. To be truly successful in education we can't be rigid and the **most inclusive teachers are the flexible ones**. It's not easy when many of us enjoy feeling in control of all that is afoot (our young people can be a touch unpredictable), but flexibility does not mean that we lose control – after all, our rules and boundaries are inflexible – but our teaching must bend to support need. You can't be accepting of 30 individual humans coming into your classroom each day, or several sets of 30 passing through it daily, if you expect to remain rigid.

That said, the changes that have occurred in more recent times have been beyond even our most fevered back-to-school nightmares, the kind that we begin to experience around 31st of August each year. These changes have had less to do with new curriculums or GCSE grade changes and endlessly revolving Education Secretaries, and more to do with the world changing. Along came the worldwide lockdowns, jauntily piggybacking onto the fact that we are currently teaching the first generation of students who both have mobile devices themselves – *and* – were raised by a generation that had mobile devices. This has made for interesting times, including the fact that attendance rates in schools consistently remain lower than pre-pandemic, with absence affecting learning, engagement, achievement, and SEMH

(Commons Library 2023). Children's relationships and interactions then have changed dramatically, both with one another and with their families.

How often do you look at **your phone**?

How much time do you spend on social media?

Do you check your phone or social media when you are in school?

Do you feel twitchy to pick your phone up soon after putting it down?

Obviously, a pandemic plus mobile phones alone are not the sole root of evil in the world (we all know teachers still believe that's Michael Gove),[2] but for our purpose here they are the 2 on which I am going to focus – because I'll bet that they are 2 on which you and your colleagues often focus, too. If you have ever tried in school or at home to get a teenager's phone off them, then you will appreciate why I am doing so. If you teach primary, then the chat you overhear between even the littlest ones often still revolves around things that they have seen or heard on a screen, not all of which is appropriate. The addiction to the mobile device and its stealthy hits of dopamine, those that make us fidgety once we've set our phones aside for 5 minutes, have caused untold drama for teachers on corridors and in lessons.

If you are currently teaching in a school, especially a secondary one, then the following list will be all too familiar:

WHICH OF THESE HAVE YOU SEEN?

- The impact of young people texting one another from different locations in the school building in order to meet up with one another – including during lesson time.
- Cruelty and bullying on social media.
- Porn on social media.
- Inappropriate photos being taken and/or sent.
- Damage to mental health and body image due to social media.
- Permanent access to inappropriate/upsetting news content on social media concerning worries such as war, climate change, and health.
- Fake news.
- Misogynistic content that has a visible effect on the ways students speak, use body language, and behave.
- Children holding phones under toilet doors whilst others use the loo – unfathomable safeguarding concerns before we even look at the emotional fallout.
- Swift passing of inappropriate material via mobile phones that is almost uncontrollable once it's out there.

2 I jest.

- Recording of teachers on mobile phones.
- Recording of other students or of fights on mobile phones, then posting on social media.
- Inciting one another to protest via social media.
- Lack of sleep due to being on mobile phones.
- Recording TikToks in the toilets/corridors.
- Charging phones using school power sockets.
- Setting up fake and damaging accounts under staff names on social media.
- Students being verbally or physically aggressive when a phone is removed.

The list could go on. Trying to have a policy in a school of possibly thousands of students whereby phones are not allowed onsite at all is simply unmanageable. Schools need implemented, consistent policies around phones, whereby they are removed when seen, but **all** staff must play their part in this. If rules are not followed, then phones can create potential nightmare scenarios and, if you work in a school, you'll know this from first-hand experience. However, worse still is the actual **physical and emotional damage** done by screen-time to children and to their social interaction skills.

Screens and Relationships

We see babies being raised by screens whilst parents are glued to their own. The expected interactions between babies and their caregivers aren't just a bit of fun, they are *absolutely crucial* to child development – without them, we risk doing real damage to our children. Access to screens that is frequent and mindless leads to babies not making connections between, for example, facial expressions and emotions. It leads to key **neural connections** not being made in their brains. They do not learn to regulate emotion and may build frustration instead (Unicef). They do not make those relational connections with their parents or carers.

How often do you see **babies or toddlers** in buggies clutching phones or devices?

Have you ever seen entire families on their phones when out for coffee, lunch or dinner?

Do you see couples on dates, both sat on their phones as opposed to **conversing**?

Which do you see more often, babies and toddlers in highchairs being occupied by their parents using books, rattles, and toys, or babies and toddlers with devices to occupy them?

None of this is said with judgment, just fact – we are most likely all guilty to some extent and to varying degrees – and avoiding blame is important. A key component to teaching is empathy, which we'll look at in more detail in Chapter 4. Parenting is hard, and we all seek ways of making life easier for ourselves. Often, it's all too easy to fall into bad habits with absolutely no intention of doing so, or even any understanding of what those habits may result in. As teachers, we need to remain as supportive of families as we can possibly be, but let's be frank as opposed to patronising one another (we are back to granny and those eggs again) and just admit that it can also be so *very hard*. This is because we're on the outside looking in, we can see the woods for the giant swathes of forest that some parents and carers find themselves trapped in, and we can therefore identify some supportive steps. It can be frustrating if a family chooses not to engage with those steps, but we still have to avoid blame – which leads only to shame.

Blaming, in the short-term, only makes *us* feel better, it's a kind of venting. What it doesn't do in the long-term is make anything better for the *child*, and if something doesn't help the child, then there's little point engaging with it anyway. What we can do, is ensure that we build and model healthy relationships ourselves with the children and young people in our classrooms.

THE STILL-FACE EXPERIMENT (SERVE AND RETURN)

Have you watched The Still-Face Experiment with Dr Edward Tronick?

The video shows a concept called 'Serve and Return', whereby a baby 'serves' (perhaps points at an object), and the caregiver – in this case, the mother – 'returns' (so looks in the direction the baby is pointing, coos, chatters). The video then shows the mother instead responding with a 'still face', giving no reactions at all, and the baby becomes more and more frustrated and upset, bewildered and desperate to regain interaction with her mummy. It is uncomfortable but powerful viewing, and quite an eye-opener. It only lasts for a minute or 2 but when we imagine that this is what some children who are then in our classes experience at home, repeatedly, then it's frightening. The 'still face' is caused by the caregiver being behind the addictive phone and perhaps ignoring the baby, and when we add in the toxic elements of children on devices and how that presents just at school, let alone at home, then where do we end up? Multiply this by our having been locked-down in a pandemic, with only our devices for company and no social interaction, and it is no wonder we are now seeing a significant rise in SEMH struggles in children, an exacerbation in mental health struggles for parents and carers, and a resulting fallout in our classrooms and schools.

Reference: Mind Your Class. (2016) *Still-Face Experiment*. [online video] Available at: www.youtube .com/watch?v=YTTSXc6sARg

---

Adverse Childhood Experiences (ACEs) and Trauma Recovery

For plenty of children, living through the pandemic may not have been an Adverse Childhood Experience (ACE). It won't have been ideal, but it won't have necessarily had a detrimental, traumatic impact. For plenty of others, it may well have been terrifying.

It was whilst I was teaching and leading in the school that was an Alternative Provision that I first received training about Maslow, about ACEs, trauma, and the practical relational pedagogies that we will look at in Chapter 4. I was amazed, upon returning to a mainstream setting, to find that very few people at the time knew about these.

Such knowledge allows us to understand more about the young people in our schools, and to really get to know them, which is so important when it comes to inclusion and children with SEND especially. When we consider Maslow and the hierarchy of needs, it teaches us that we must be mindful about what is happening for, or to, that child outside of the school gates. We have to consider what they are coming to us with in terms of experience and in terms of possible trauma. These days, there is far more training going on within particular local authorities and mainstream settings than when I first returned to one a few years ago, and this is in direct response to the changes in teaching and society that we have discussed, and because relational approaches are proving to be so successful.

ACEs include but are not limited to:

- Physical abuse.
- Sexual abuse.
- Emotional abuse.
- Living with a family member who has a mental illness or poor mental health.
- Living with a family member with substance abuse issues (alcohol, drugs, prescription medication and so on).
- Living with a family member who has addictions such as gambling that affects family relationships and finances.
- Having a family member who is in prison or involved with crime.
- Having no stable home to live in.
- Being exposed to domestic violence.
- The death of a parent.

Statistically, people who have experienced **4 or more ACEs** have a significantly increased risk of, for example, substance misuse, depression, teenage pregnancy, unemployment, and (due to the impact on their behaviours, lifestyle, and SEMH) premature death. The more ACEs a person experiences, the worse their outcomes may be. There is also statistical data to show that these children may well, in a **cyclic effect**, raise children of *their own* who are in turn exposed to a higher number of ACEs (Bellis et al. 2014).

Due to the nature of our profession, we are the frontline for these children and, therefore, we can do something about it to make their lives and their outcomes better. Of course, we do not necessarily always know that children are experiencing, for example, abuse, and you will have been trained to know that safeguarding is everyone's responsibility, but this also backs up why we should, no matter what, treat all young people with **kindness**. Again, this does not mean being a soft touch. Again, it's about being firm with clear boundaries and high expectations, but being firm does not mean that you cannot remain calm, modelling respect, whilst also challenging behaviours that aren't acceptable – and remembering to both try to *seek and support* the **cause** of the **effect**, thereby positively influencing the outcome of the latter.

Readily Available Trusted Adults (That's Us!)

In the midst of thinking about the challenging life experiences that some of our children and young people live with, there is heart-warming news. Further research has been shown to evidence that if those who suffer a number of ACEs have even just *one trusted adult* who believes in them, and who encourages and supports them to believe in *themselves*, then their entire outlook and outcomes can change.

Obviously, the best scenario is that this adult is a parent, or preferably both parents, but by the very nature of ACEs, this is often not the case. However, the reparation therefore can very often come from teachers. You, us, we – are in the position to truly change not only that child's life, but the lives of their own future children which, as the data shows us, may otherwise be adversely affected by the childhood experiences that were out of the control of their own traumatised parents.

You will have children in your classroom who have experienced ACEs. They may well present differently to one another, depending on what support they have received, who looks after them, and also because of the relationship you have with them.

We all need trusted adults when we're children. Can you identify a readily available trusted adult from your own childhood who supported you or made a difference to your life?

What made them different to other adults? How did you know you could trust them?

According to a study that took place in 2017, having a trusted adult led to deeper resilience in young people, which itself led to their ability to negate some of the toxic effects of particular ACEs and traumatic experiences (Ashton et al. 2021). Even people who had experienced more than 4 ACEs were shown to be nearly 6 times more likely to go on to form relationships and supportive friendships and to develop the life skills needed to succeed when they had a **trusted adult who was readily available**. We see again then that crucial element of trust which links back to **unconditional positive regard**, because if a child or young person is not treated with that, then are they likely to trust us? No. And if they do not trust us, and they therefore do not have access to a trusted adult, are they as likely to succeed in life? I think we know the answer to this one.

I began this book by mentioning my own experiences of the loss of a parent, but this was not the only adverse childhood experience that I went through and lived with as a child. None of these are appropriate nor relevant to go into here, however, the strong belief that both my mother and my grandfather had in me, and my complete childhood trust in them, made a monumental difference to how I coped with the ACEs that I experienced and the person that I eventually became.

You may well be reading this yourself recognising experiences that you had as a child. You may even, as I once did when I first encountered the term 'ACEs' in a training session, have suddenly experienced the lightbulb moment of thinking, 'What? *That was* **me**?' When we experience those moments as adults, it can be shocking. If we have been lucky enough to develop resilience and to come out the other side to healthy adulthood, especially with no form of intervention in between, then it can shake us to the core to realise that there are names for what we experienced and went through as kids. That there are studies about it, and statistics, and data that now underpins trauma-informed responses in schools. This can be both self-affirming and triggering, and it's wise to remember the importance of your own wellbeing again, and having your needs met before you can attend to those of others. *Look after yourself.*

So, as teachers, we are in the privileged position of being able to support children and young people and to make the difference that we came into teaching for. The 'difference' is perhaps clichéd but who cares? Because, as with most clichés, it is absolutely true.

What About Attachment Disorders?

To begin wrapping up Chapter 3, if we think back to the SEND Code of Practice and the descriptor of SEMH needs, then it includes the term 'attachment disorder'. This is a bit of an umbrella term that encapsulates and refers to a variety of emotional or behavioural conditions that involve a child or young person's ability (or inability) to form healthy, emotional attachments to their caregivers, or parents, in infancy. Now that we have an understanding of ACEs, childhood trauma, the process of Serve and Return and so forth, we are hopefully able to understand how attachment issues lay within, and arise from, these early childhood experiences of interaction (or lack thereof). Again, it all comes down to **relationships.**

There are some schools of thought that suggest we can identify several different types of attachment disorder and others that put it more simply, in terms of children forming either 'secure attachments' or 'insecure attachments'. It is fairly self-explanatory that the former is the more positive and ideal kind of attachment for infants to forge, and the latter is that which may lead instead to a child presenting with distress, anxiety, and an inability to engage with others or form healthy, trusting relationships. Infants who form insecure attachments are more likely to have not been made to feel safe and secure by their caregivers – let us think back to the Serve and Return, or the parents and carers who themselves experienced ACEs but had no readily available, trusted adult. Let us consider the pandemic and how it changed the ways in which we interact, or socialise, or the fact that many of us now spend our time behind screens. Let us think back to Maslow and the basic needs of children being met.

We've done our groundwork here so we can place attachment disorders in this context – and we can see how crucial relationships are to both the child in infancy, the child in school, and the adult that the child will become. Everything is about relationships. And everything that we have looked at so far in this book has directed us to the understanding that **relationships are the starting point**. They are our foundation and your relationships in school are going to be what you build your classroom upon.

So, let's progress to Chapter 4, and look in more detail at the **4 relational pedagogies** that are going to help you to do so.

PART 2: THE 'WHY' OF RELATIONAL APPROACHES

Takeaways

- Children's **most basic needs** are not always being met before they come into our classrooms.
- We need to consider **cause and effect** to help us find and support those needs, so that children can be ready to learn.
- SEMH needs are rising.
- Trust must be **built and earned**.
- Removing children from learning does **not** build trust, support the child, nor make a positive difference to them.
- The realities of classrooms in the 21st century make the **modelling and building** of relationships more important than ever.
- Screentime, devices, and lockdowns have **negatively impacted** children and damaged their development of social, emotional, and relational skills.
- Factors in the lives of children that are out of our control may mean that they are in real need of a **readily available trusted adult** to make the difference in their lives.
- Making that difference to a child's life may also very well mean making a difference to the lives of their **future generations**.

COMING UP NEXT

- **Chapter 4** will consider the **how** of **relational approaches** - detailing 4 pedagogies to use as the foundation on which your inclusive classroom will stand, including practical ideas and guidance.

Out of the Mouths of Staff

Covid seems to have impacted the social skills of the children. The way they talk to each other is not nice at times, but they are used to hiding behind screens and did a lot of this during the pandemic. This has led to an inability for some to interact socially. I think the social skills aspect is the biggest issue – there has definitely been a decline in these through both mobiles and covid.

Inclusion Lead, Seniors

I think the biggest impact of Covid-19 has been on students' resilience and social skills. There are so many issues with friendships and the way the kids speak to one another. This is then strongly linked to ability to cope with challenge and difficult situations, and subsequently we've seen a rise in SEMH needs.

Teacher, All-Through School

I think one of the best things that you can do for the children is to ensure your classroom is a safe space. Model respect, recognise that you have to earn it. Realise that yelling gets you nowhere. These kids don't pop along ready to trust us like it's the 1950s, they're exposed to goodness knows what on social media. They don't automatically care that we are 'teachers'. We have to be recognised instead as humans – and recognise the same in them.

Class Teacher, Primary

We have a massive issue with kids vaping in the toilets. We're a lovely school in a leafy area, great families, not especially challenging behaviour, but the vaping! It's a huge issue. The vapes look like toys which doesn't help, they don't set our alarms off (good job, we'd be outside 90% of the time), and it's far easier for the young people to get away with vaping than smoking. Vapes even smell like body sprays. I have no idea how we'll ever get on top of it to be honest.

Assistant Headteacher, Secondary

References

Ashton, K., Davies, A.R., Hughes, K., Ford, K., Cotter-Roberts, A., and Bellis, M.A. (2021). Adult support during childhood: A retrospective study of trusted adult relationships, sources of personal adult support and their association with childhood resilience resources. *BMC Psychology*, 9(1), p. 101. http://doi.og/10.1186/s40359-021-00601-x. PMID: 34176519; PMCID: PMC8237477

Bellis, M., Lowey, H., Leckenby, N., Hughes, K., and Harrison, D. (2014). Adverse childhood experiences: Retrospective study to determine their impact on adult health behaviours and health outcomes in a UK population. *Journal of Public Health*, 36(1), pp. 81–91. Available at: https://doi.org/10.1093/pubmed/fdt038

Blanden, J., Crawford, C., Fumagalli, L., and Rabe, B. (2021). School Closures and Children's Emotional and Behavioural Difficulties [online]. Available at: https://mk0nuffieldfounpg9ee.kinstacdn.com/wp-content/uploads/2020/10/School-closures-andchildrens-emotional-and-behavioural-difficulties.pdf

Cherry, K. (2020). *Unconditional Positive Regard in Psychology*. Available at: www.verywellmind.com/what-is-unconditional-positive-regard-2796005

Commons Library. (2023). Available at: https://commonslibrary.parliament.uk/research-briefings/cbp-9710/

Maslow, A. (1943). A Theory of Human Motivation. *Psychological Review*, 50(4), pp. 370–396.

Mind Your Class. (2016) *Still-Face Experiment* [online video]. Available at: www.youtube.com/watch?v=YTTSXc6sARg

Perry, P. (2019). *The Book You Wish Your Parents Had Read (and Your Children Will Be Glad That You Did)*. Penguin Life.

SEND Network. (2023). Available at: https://send-network.co.uk/posts/policy-context-social-emotional-and-mental-health-needs

Special Educational Needs in England. (2023). Available at: https://explore-education-statistics.service.gov.uk/find-statistics/special-educational-needs-in-england#dataBlock-b88fbba0-6fbe-4100-1661-08da47b0392d-charts

The Harvard Gazette. (2017). Available at: https://news.harvard.edu/gazette/story/2017/04/over-nearly-80-years-harvard-study-has-been-showing-how-to-live-a-healthy-and-happy-life/

Unicef. Available at: https://www.unicef.org/parenting/child-development/babies-screen-time#:~:text=Exposure%20to%20screens%20reduces%20babies,and%20interacting%20with%20other%20children

Whitaker, D. (2021). *The Kindness Principle: Making Relational Behaviour Management Work in Schools*. Independent Thinking Press.

Chapter Four

The 'How' of Relational Approaches

Four Core Approaches with Which to Build Your Foundation

We just wouldn't be teachers if we didn't begin this chapter by recapping our prior learning. So, in Chapter 3, we examined:

- The '**what**' of relational approaches – what they are and what they are not, as well as looking at how supportive they are for all children, and especially those with SEMH needs.

And we also considered:

- The '**why**' of relational approaches – why they matter and why they are *needed*, putting the reasons into context via exploring the needs of children and young people in 21st-century classrooms.

This chapter then will detail:

- The '**how**' of relational approaches, presented in four parts, as we move on to consider how you can use them to build your inclusive classroom's solid foundation. The 4 pedagogies are:

	Relational Pedagogy	*Summary*
Part 1	**Emotional Intelligence**	How to use our emotional intelligence in our classrooms and around our schools.
Part 2	**Nurture**	The 6 Principles of Nurture and how to embed them in our classrooms, underpinned by emotional intelligence.
Part 3	**Restorative (or Relational) Practice**	How restorative practice can change culture and ethos, underpinned by emotional intelligence.
Part 4	**PACE (Playfulness, Acceptance, Curiosity and Empathy)**	How employing a PACE approach allows young people to feel safe in our classrooms, and to flourish, underpinned by emotional intelligence.

DOI: 10.4324/b23417-5

You'll see when we look at these how you can incorporate aspects into your practice to build that solid relational foundation. These 4 pedagogies will help you to adapt your responses and approaches to different children with different needs and, because of the concepts that we have explored so far, you also know and understand **why** you need to do so. Everything that we have discussed and examined so far in the book, will now begin to come together to form the unshakeable bedrock of your inclusive classroom. Remember that the key of consistency will let you in, and let's be mindful of our model of **cause and effect** as we move forwards.

Remember **why** these approaches are needed.

Do all children come to school automatically **trusting** us?

Have all children's most **basic needs** been met before they join us?

Are children always treated with **unconditional positive regard** in school, no matter who they are, how they behave, and where they are coming from?

Part 1

Emotional Intelligence

We are going to begin, as all things should, with emotional intelligence. This will be the shorter of these four sections, but it is key to everything else that will be incorporated in your sturdy relational foundation.

Everything in your classroom should be **underpinned** by emotional intelligence. I know that there can be a propensity for some to sigh and give a practised eyeroll upon hearing this term, but if we are not in touch with how we and others **feel**, given that our feelings are entirely integral to being human, driving many of our behaviours, then we are a lost cause. We cannot appreciate or empathise with a child who simply cannot access the work in our classroom if we have no concept of how they might in that case feel (miserable), or how it might make us feel (joyous) if we are able to support them. Our **actions are motivated by our emotions**, and children and young people even more so.

Can you think of **colleagues** at your school who are emotionally intelligent?

Can you think of some who are **not**?

How do you know that they are/are not?

What **effect** does this have on both yourself and the students?

How About Emotional Intelligence in Schools?

In an ideal world, your school will be led by people who are themselves emotionally intelligent. (**Does your SLT come across this way?**) Leadership at best incorporates and draws from a variety of styles. Successful leadership is never about only being autocratic (heaven forbid), or only being collaborative, or only being authoritative. No doubt we've all worked for that one entirely autocratic leader, whether in teaching or before we entered the profession. The one who clicked their fingers in your direction and ordered you where to go and what to do. Who very much engaged in only ever doing things *to* staff and never *with* staff due to their own massively inflated ego. Who probably only ever inspired you to come up with witty nicknames about them behind their backs and to keep the local job page open on your phone at all times.

A leader has to inspire, positively, and if they aren't emotionally intelligent then the chances are that the most they'll encourage are choice expletives muttered darkly in unhappy staffrooms. The entirely autocratic leader never builds relationships with their staff because they don't think they need to; they are not emotionally intelligent. They believe people should just do as they're told. Ditto for the autocratic teacher, who will have just as little success in their subcommunity of the classroom as the autocratic head will, over the long-term, in the larger community of the school.

This idea of doing things – that we may sometimes morally disagree with – just because we are told to is in itself a can of worms. If we think of the infamous (and deeply unethical) **Stanley Milgram** experiment, which looked at the willingness of people to carry out sometimes horrific tasks just because a person in **authority** instructed them to, then it is reminiscent of the corporal punishment model of past classrooms. Milgram's volunteers actually believed that they were administering high voltage electric shocks to people (who were in fact actors pretending to be shocked), and despite how upset some of the volunteers were at doing so, they still did it – even whilst the actors screamed.

Back in the teaching days of yore, staff could throw board rubbers at children. They could beat them, whip them with canes, or rulers, or slippers. It is *unthinkable* sitting here now to even contemplate doing this, let alone agreeing because we've been told to. These days we support traumatised children, we certainly do not attempt to traumatise them ourselves. I remember being terrified aged four and starting school because of rumours that abounded even in pre-schools about canes and sticks. Astoundingly, it was not until 1986 that corporal punishment was legally abolished within UK-maintained schools.[1] 1986. Nor of course did it cure all of society's ills. Funny that. So, if beating kids with canes and terrifying them into compliance – the very definition of doing *to* as opposed to *with* didn't 'work', then we can see that **punitive punishment** won't either.

Did teachers inflict physical punishment on children as a result of **temper**, or to breed **compliance** out of fear?

Did they only attempt to achieve compliance this way because **SLT** told them to?

Who took **moral accountability** for corporal punishment in schools? And what was the **emotional effect** on all involved?

Emotional intelligence is most definitely about working *with*. **Daniel Goleman**, internationally respected for his work on leadership and emotional intelligence, advocates that the latter is the core thread that runs through inclusion (Goleman 2011). Without it then, we run the risk of the whole shebang – our classroom, our school, our ethos – unravelling. Goleman's work on leadership can be applied just as well to class teaching and, particularly, **adaptive teaching**. We have to adapt our approaches according to our current vision and what we want to achieve, relative to the circumstances.

If we only tell students to 'do what we say because we tell you to and because we are teachers', are we going to be successful? Let's be honest. For the majority of expectation-abiding students, then yes, because of compliance – though because it's purely through compliance, it's not going to be especially meaningful. For those students with a variety of needs, it is far less likely. For students with SEMH needs, or even just rampaging hormones, absolutely not. Children need to understand the reason for rules, so that they can value them and make informed and better choices, both in and outside of school. And anyway, just because you **can** do something, it doesn't mean you **should**. For all students, working with them is better than doing things to them. There will always be times when we have to tell a student what to do – especially for their safety or that of others – but putting people and their feelings first, using unconditional positive regard, and urging them to come with us of their own good choice-making ability, is so much better for all involved. In order to achieve this, we'll look further on in this chapter at the work of **Mark Finnis**, **Marshall Rosenberg**, and **Dan Seigel**.

Good leaders, and good teachers, make changes where change is necessary, reflecting in-action, and not only on-action. This is an 'extremely efficient method of reflection' that allows us to reflect during an event and, subsequently, change the outcome as the event occurs (Cambridge Assessment). This, when combined with an affiliative approach, can be highly productive. For example, when you find yourself in challenging meetings and you are able to follow the need and mood of the room, pre-empting outcomes and working for success. It can also be highly productive as a class teacher because, as such, you are leading the room. *This* is your bread and butter – this is part and parcel of adaptive teaching. Using your emotional intelligence to not only lead but to read the room. Reading body language as well as we read the written word, and reacting appropriately to it, is how we adapt the lesson in the very midst of said lesson, thereby changing the learning success for the young people in it.

In essence, **do not be afraid** of emotional intelligence. As with all relational approaches, this is not about being a soft touch. **Kindness isn't weakness**. But empathising (as we'll explore when we look at **PACE** a little further on) is absolutely crucial to understanding and getting to know the children in our schools, responding to their needs, and adapting our teaching and our approaches accordingly.

The 'How To'

How to Use Emotional Intelligence in Your Classroom

Try this:	By doing this:
Incorporate SEAL (Social, Emotional Aspects of Learning) in your classroom. The five strands of SEAL are: Self-awareness Managing Feelings Motivation Empathy Social skills	**Try a SEAL learning outcome as well as an academic one. This can be whole-class or personalised and discrete. Normalise emotions.** 'Today we are going to feel pride in our work and we shall show it!' 'By the end of our lesson, we are each going to have listened carefully to one another'. 'I shall be able to identify when I am feeling frustrated'.
Be explicit with body language.	**E.g. Careful use of facial expression – what are you trying to convey?** Silent disapproval to gently manage behaviour, joy to instil pride, energy to motivate, sympathy to encourage emotional engagement. Be mindful. Make eye contact, encourage with others when they are able. Smile like you mean it!
Encourage empathy explicitly.	**Be explicit about a situation that requires empathy and why, and how that might feel.** Watching a newsreel about a natural disaster, how might people in the video feel? How might we feel watching it? What does empathy motivate us to do, such as charitable acts? Is empathy always comfortable? Would we want people to empathise with us? Why?
Careful use of language.	**Use the language of 'we' and 'us'.** Give students some ownership of the classroom, of teamwork, of camaraderie. We are in it together. They are just as worthy of respect as teachers are. We are all as valuable as one another.
Model calm, model respect.	**Remember our unconditional positive regard.** Model it. Use your voice but don't lose it – never shout, rely instead on intonation when needed. Always be polite, always be respectful, make the children feel safe even when dealing with tricky situations.
Speaking and listening activities.	**Ensure the students feel listened to and heard, and ensure they listen to and hear one another.** This enables people to feel valued, worthwhile, that their opinions matter. Plan in activities that allow this.
Give *time*.	**Show students that they are worth your time.** It's easy to turn students away sometimes. I have seen some go to find teachers at lunchtime only to see the teacher, behind the glass of their classroom door, tell the child that they are having their lunch and to go away – with no 'come back in 5 minutes' or 'come back at 3pm', just 'go away'. Give children your time.

PART 1: EMOTIONAL INTELLIGENCE

Takeaways

- Being emotionally intelligent is not a weakness; it's a **strength**.
- Being emotionally intelligent means doing things **with** people, not **to** them.
- Remember a time when you have been treated without emotional intelligence and devalued. How did you **feel**? Was it motivating?
- We can get **better results** out of all people, children and adults alike, if we use our emotional intelligence.
- Daniel Goleman is a key proponent of emotional intelligence as a **central tenet** of inclusion.
- Incorporating **SEAL** in our classrooms explicitly models emotional intelligence to the children and young people within them.

Part 2

Nurture

Question: Do You *Nurture* the Young People in Your Classroom?

I suspect most of us would say yes. I hope so. It is by no means rocket science to assume that when we nurture something, or someone, it or they go on to have more chance of flourishing than withering on the vine. There is possibly a tendency in some secondary schools, perhaps, to assume that nurturing is more the role of our primary and Early Years specialists. Or, to go a step further, maybe the role of parents, with less consideration for how we as teachers should also be nurturing those 6-foot, sometimes gobby 16-year-olds just as much as we should the tiddlers in Year R. To 'nurture' means of course to care for something, to tend to it. According to one definition, it also means to *cherish* (OED 2016).

Cue Another Question: Do You *Cherish* the Young People in Your Classroom?

If you are being 100% honest with yourself, can you still answer in the affirmative? I am willing to bet that fewer of us would say we actively *cherish the children* than would say we nurture them – but these terms are synonymous. If we agree that we should nurture them, then we should, by definition, cherish them. I'll just leave that thought there. If we couple it with unconditional positive regard (UPR), then it does begin to make more sense. Less so when we are trying to extract an especially stubborn child from a toilet in which they've chosen to hide, but perhaps this is also the exact time to be mindful of our cherishment, and to employ said regard?

> Can you think now of a couple of students whom you find it **hard** to nurture?
>
> **Why** do you find it hard? (For example, they wind you up, they're rude, you then engage in being sarcastic.)
>
> **How** then can you address this and overcome it, in order to always treat those young people with UPR? (Silent mantra, deep breaths, being mindful of why you should.)
>
> Alternatively, can you think of students whom you **actively nurture**? What's the difference? Why is it easier to nurture some more than others, what do we need to change in order to be more consistent?

How About Nurture in Schools?

You may, especially if you are a primary specialist, work in, or have worked in, schools that have a Nurture Provision. This might be less likely, though certainly not unheard of, if you're based in a secondary school. In fact, in some areas of the UK, secondary schools have developed a whole-school approach to Nurture as a concept. Before we look at that, let's look at what Nurture actually is.

Traditionally, the concept of 'Nurture' in education links to **Marjorie Boxall** and her work that originated in the 1970s and it is based around SEMH and Social and Emotional Aspects of Learning (SEAL). Boxall first founded Nurture Groups in response to impoverished areas of society and, because of this, it is crucial when suggesting that children may benefit from access to a Nurture Group that careful communications are upheld with parents and, when this is successful, parents can recognise it as a positive experience. It is also important to recognise that a lack of material goods and money, does obviously not equate to a lack of Nurture.

Nurture Groups are essentially an intervention. Children will be referred to them by class teachers and specialist Nurture staff will complete what is known as a **Boxall Profile** about the child, providing a baseline if you like of the child's needs, and meaning that progress can be measured. Now, admittedly, for those of us who like hard data, then an intervention based upon SEMH does not equate to the kind that a numeracy intervention propagates. However, this does not mean that we cannot (or should not) support the emotional needs of children. As with emotional intelligence, it is a language that some of us can find a bit fluffy, but we simply cannot get away from the fact that our emotions fuel our actions and our thoughts. They are a driving force.

Nurture as a provision has been positively reviewed by the inspectors-that-shall-not-be-named (Ofsted 2011), and a review of SEMH interventions that was published by Babcock LDP in 2018 acknowledges that it is helpful to amalgamate a variety of approaches, such as Nurture, as part of our educationalist 'toolkit' (Babcock LDP 2018).

The point then of us looking at Nurture here is because you can use what are known as the **6 Principles of Nurture** to underpin your inclusive classroom. These principles were developed by educationalists **Eva Holmes** and **Eve Boyd** in 1999 in response to Boxall's work, and we can put them to good use by being mindful of them in our classrooms (Nurture UK). If we consider our earlier discussions in Chapter 3 around children with attachment disorders or those who have suffered trauma, then it is also helpful to note that the concept of Nurture (and therefore access to provisions, schools or classrooms that are underpinned by it) is seen as being especially supportive for children with **complex attachment needs**.

The 'How To'

How to Use Nurture in Your Classroom

If we are to apply these 6 Principles then to our classrooms, we need to consider what each looks like. I mentioned that in various areas in the UK, local authorities have implemented Nurture across schools. They have developed auditing tools, frameworks, and supportive guidance regarding how to do so; for example, the Royal Society for the Arts (RSA), supported by the Mayor of London, produced a toolkit in 2021 for 'Inclusion and Nurture' that worked towards reducing exclusions (RSA 2021). In Scotland, a framework was developed for using Nurture as a whole-school approach, so that we move beyond the Nurture Group, to establishing these principles across whole schools, in each classroom and beyond (Applying Nurture as a Whole-School Approach 2017).

Let's discuss therefore what this looks like for you. According to www.nurtureuk.org, the principles are as follows. I have included some descriptors and space for you to do a mini-audit of your own practice:

Nurture principle	What that looks like	How can you incorporate this? How do you already?
Children's learning is understood developmentally.	Respond to children's **developmental progress** and not just their traditional attainment levels. Remember when we looked at Maslow and being **future-ready**, not necessarily MENSA-ready? Be mindful of that here. **Accept** who the child is (and this will link to PACE approaches that we will look at a little later on in this chapter). **Avoid judging** children, **avoid blaming** anyone. Model **respect.** Maintain high expectations but ensure they are **achievable and relative** to the child and who they are.	

Nurture principle	What that looks like	How can you incorporate this? How do you already?
The classroom offers a safe base.	Remember that key of **consistency**. Have clear routines that are visible where possible, have structure so that students know what to expect and feel safe within those boundaries. Consider having a 'Smart Start' **routine** and a visual of it, for example, setting out high expectations for entry to your room (greeting at the door, stand behind chairs, get equipment out and so on - reverse procedure at the end). Use the **UPR** that we have discussed and be mindful about doing so. Be a source of reliability for the young people. Model that. **Never** humiliate students, use your emotional intelligence. Remember working *with* and not doing *to*. Get to know the children, pay **attention** to them, **know their needs**. **Take nothing for granted**; remember Maslow and trust, recall our '**cause** and **effect**' model from earlier in this chapter. Recognise if you are about to escalate a situation - it's ok to ask another adult to provide a brief 'change of face' if needed. Be that **readily available trusted adult** - work towards that trust. Show you're worthy of it.	
The importance of nurture for the development of wellbeing.	Remember Chapter 1 when we spoke about our own wellbeing? It's no different for the student and because we are leading our classrooms from a position of emotional intelligence, we know this. It's that **core thread** running through inclusion. **Value** the children, listen to them and ensure that they know they are heard. Consider how you speak to them - UPR - and think about how what comes out of your mouth is going to 'land' on them. Use the language of '**us, we, together**', create a supportive vibe, a room in which you work with and not do to. Ask after the children. Get to know their interests. Remember **Maslow** - are you meeting needs, does the child trust you? Can somebody help you in doing so? Avoid the **ejector seat**. Look at and try to support the **causes** of the **effects**. Acknowledge and celebrate success in a **personalised** way; if a student doesn't like public attention, do it discretely and so on.	

Nurture principle	What that looks like	How can you incorporate this? How do you already?
Language is a vital means of communication.	Be aware of your **body language** and how you are setting a tone through not just your voice but your entire physicality in the classroom. Be aware of the children's body language. Be aware of what their behaviour is **communicating,** especially if their speech and language is a need. Use **circle time** with all age groups (more of this in Chapter 5). Model what you expect to see – when something is handed to you, say 'thank you'. Then if the student does not say, for example, 'you're welcome', **gently encourage** them to do so. Hold doors open and model manners as someone passes through. Do this **explicitly with staff**, too. When bells ring or at lesson changeover, if you're in a secondary setting, stand out on the corridor greeting students, be a **positive presence** modelling positive use of language to communicate how we feel.	
All behaviour is communication.	This can be a tricky one because teachers can spend hours arguing over whether behaviour is a need or a choice. Depending on who a student is and what their needs are, it can be either. What this does not take away from however, is that *all of our behaviour communicates something*. Think back to **emotional intelligence**; our behaviours are driven by how we feel. If we are furious (**emotion**) we may slam a door (**behaviour**). If our headteacher perpetually does things *to* us as opposed to working *with* us, we may feel quiet rage (emotion) and show this by sticking 2 fingers up at their back as they stalk away from us (behaviour). The difference is, because we are adults, there is an expectation that we have better control over our behaviours, hence the fact that we don't stick our fingers up directly in the face of the headteacher but do it in a more regulated and sly manner than might a raging 10-year-old. Remember Maslow and trust, remember our model of **cause and effect** – and that we must get to and support the root cause, and remember that we must respond with **UPR**. Also – ignore the ejector seat. If we do not deal with this ourselves, from a **relational standpoint**, it will never progress and we cannot truly support whatever the child is trying to communicate to us.	

Nurture principle	What that looks like	How can you incorporate this? How do you already?
	Give students the chance to explain what has happened, empathise, let the child calm down before you begin to speak, remember your body language, use **non-verbal empathy** where you can, use **distraction** if a situation is escalating, **hold regulation** for the child in the **safe space** of your classroom (explicitly tell them you are there to support them, that you are there to help).	
The importance of transition in children's lives.	This is massive. Plenty of the children that you teach will not like change, whether they have any additional needs or not, but since 2020 they have had to adapt and try to cope with **monumental changes**. There have been changes that we as adults have found challenging. Also of course, there will be plenty of us as adults who found it horrendous to be bandied about on the pandemic rollercoaster, and this will be the same for parents and carers. Children will have seen the adults around them being scared and unsure, leading to those children feeling unsafe around change. So we can empathise with the young people in our schools. Our **entire world changed**, not just our year group or our teacher – and remember that some of our young people don't even like the change of going from one room to the next. So, maintain that **safe space** of your classroom, keep turning that key of consistency and remember again to also maintain those boundaries and expectations. If a child needs support **managing transitions**, then speak to your SENDCO too. It's especially helpful if you are **preventative** as opposed to reactive, and do seek parent or carer support when needed, too.	

So, we build our inclusive classroom as a safe, consistent learning space, where children are understood in terms of their **developmental progress** and not just their academic achievement. We do so using and modelling our emotional intelligence as well as our more traditional subject knowledge – because, after all, we are teaching humans, not little rows of robotics – and we make no assumptions about the children before they join us. We do not assume that they trust us, or that they have been taught how and why to behave appropriately, or that they have some of their most basic needs met. We are open to adapting our **approaches** and not only our lessons.

PART 2: NURTURE

Takeaways

- There are **6 Principles** of Nurture.
- **Nurture Groups** take place as timetabled interventions whereby needs are 'assessed' using a Boxall Profile.
- Nurture as a **concept** has been used as a **whole-school approach** in various successful studies.
- Nurture as a concept is **easily employed** in our classrooms.
- **All children**, whether they have experienced Adverse Childhood Experiences (ACEs) for example or not, or whether they have SEND or not, will benefit from this approach.
- Nurture is about using our **emotional intelligence** and being **child-centred**.

Part 3

Restorative (or Relational) Practice

Restorative or Relational Practice are one and the same, and they form a core part of your inclusive classroom's solid foundation. Let's call them RP for ease of language.

In this section, we will look at three practical strategies to create a restorative, relational culture in your classroom:

1) The Social Discipline Window
2) Nonviolent Communication and Speaking with the Children
3) Name It to Tame It – How to Help Children Manage Emotions

Before we do this, some background on RP is essential – and provides fascinating insight regarding how it works.

RP is the **antithesis of the ejector seat** (see Chapter 3). It is the opposite of exclusion. Some people may assume that RP is the easy, soft, weak option – but actually, this is the tougher option. RP is about **high challenge** – it's not about letting kids run amok and trying to be pals with them. But it's also about **high support**. It takes a lot longer to change a culture than it does to kick kids out of classrooms. But the former makes for children and young people who enter the wider world being future-ready, understanding more about themselves and what makes them tick, about what regulates them, and how to aspire to be the best that they can be. The latter makes for a short-term and, frankly, unethical solution.

We have already established that relationships are our starting point. The aforementioned Harvard study (Chapter 3) found not only that healthy, strong relationships make us happier (obvious) but also that they lead to better *physical* health too – more so than money, fame, and power. This tells us that even having the money to access better health care, for example, does not positively affect our physical health to the same extent as the relationships we forge along the way. Most likely, this is down to those relationships resulting in lower stress levels, stronger emotional connections, better care for ourselves and being cared for by others, and so on. In essence, the relationship is the **cause**, and longer, happier lives are the **effect**. To progress to attaining anything else in life, we have to build strong relationships. In a world where our social connections took a bit of a battering thanks to a pandemic, and where many of our young people now live their lives out behind screens as opposed to connecting in-person, this is more important than ever.

Relationships make all the difference in our lives.

Can you describe a **healthy** relationship?

Can you describe an **unhealthy** one?

What relationships do you have in school that **support** you?

Can you **identify the students** with whom you have a strong relationship compared to some with whom you do not? What is making the difference, and what can you do about it? Indeed, what are you *willing* to do about it?

Relationships and Family Dynamics

When I was a teenager, in a world far, far away from the teens of today, I was only allowed out on certain nights of the week. (I got to choose the nights, so I guess I felt a part of the process.) This was in a time when landlines were still the sole form of telecommunication indoors. I would leave school in the afternoon, get the bus home with my friend, Cath, and then once I was indoors, I'd immediately ring Cath from the aforementioned landline. Without realising it, I was practising my speaking and listening skills, my social and emotional skills, my ability to both move a conversation forwards and respond appropriately to someone else's views and opinions. Obviously, our mothers would complain on either side, phone-bill dependent, questioning why we felt the need to ring each other after an entire day in school plus a bus ride home together (the never-ending mystery of what there could 'possibly be left to talk about'), but they this did with teasing endearment.

On those evenings, there was then the unwritten expectation that I'd do some homework, eat with my lovely mum, have a good chat about our days, and then maybe snuggle up and watch Inspector Morse at 9pm on a Wednesday. So, much as there was a screen involved later in the day, there was, prior to that, an entire day's worth of schooling, eating together as a family, socialising and relaxing as a family, and socialising and relaxing with friends. Skip forwards to the 21st century, and whilst working with a group of 10-year-olds recently, 6 out of the 10 told me that they **did not eat together** with their family in the evening. They each went to different rooms with their meals, to either watch their own TVs, go on their phones, or engage in gaming. Others said they did sit together ... but on their phones. And this is a common picture. I do not say this with judgement, but as fact.

Do you know how many of your students sit down and **eat with their families** at night?

Don't be afraid to gently suggest **eating together** to families who don't, using your emotional intelligence, or asking your SENDCO to support you in doing so. Studies show that eating together makes a real difference.

The change in relational dynamics across the past couple of decades, then, is huge. One study from 2015 deduced that frequent family meals lead to better **self-esteem** and **school success**, whereas a lack of was associated with disordered eating, substance misuse, and depression (Harrison et al. 2015). (Remember those **cyclic ACEs**.) The simple act of eating together, whether we have a table to do so at or not, encourages that feeling of nurture, of warmth, of togetherness. If we think back to Nurture as a concept and of Nurture Groups, a key part of them is often the act of eating together. Children setting the table, making toast, patiently sharing the butter, with adults modelling conversation, etiquette, and social skills. If we consider that plenty of our young people today are lacking this, it's incredibly sad – and we then, again, are that **reparation** in the classroom. As teachers we can be the readily accessible trusted adult. We can stand our classrooms firm upon restorative, relational practice and high expectation.

How About Restorative/Relational Practice in Schools?

RP, you won't be surprised to hear, is grounded in **consistency**. It's not a behaviour management system but a **change of culture** – and this culture is what we want embedded in our inclusive classroom. Whether RP is embedded as whole-school practice will be for SLT to decide but we can all incorporate it personally. It is excellent practice for supporting SEMH across schools but, as with adaptive teaching, it is also excellent practice for supporting all students – and adults. RP is grounded upon the theory that punitive approaches, those 'punishments' we spoke about earlier, only contain the behaviour. They do not *change* it – think about our model of **cause and effect** here. RP is a way of working *with* people and not doing *to*, which has been a theme that has run through all that we have examined so far.

We sometimes seem to separate 'teaching', as a concept, from 'behaviour management' as a concept. I would argue instead that 'teaching' should automatically incorporate teaching better behaviours. It is not about purely academic outcomes. We are back to that cry of 'we just want to teach!' – but what do we want to teach? If it's just *insert academic outcome here*, then that's not what 'teaching' is. When that's what we think it is, and that's what we allow it to become in our classrooms, then that's when things go pear-shaped. Teaching is **holistic**: better behaviour, subject knowledge and skill sets, passion, social skills, relationships, and so on.

What did '**teaching**' mean to you *before* you became a teacher?

What did it mean when you *first* became a teacher?

Depending on how long you've taught and where, does it mean something different to you *now*?

Crime and Punishment (and Why the Latter Does Not Work)

When we think of our criminal justice system, it follows a similar pattern to our behaviour systems in schools. There is a sliding scale, or a ladder, of **incremental consequences** for actions and behaviour. When we considered the doomed ejector seat in Chapter 3, we also considered, correspondingly, the '3 strikes and you're out' system that some schools employ – and why this does not work in the long-term. We looked at not confusing 'meaning-ful consequences' with 'punitive punishments', although plenty of schools do, and plenty of teachers believe children are deserving of the latter. But does this thinking, and the result-ing practice, work?

In our criminal justice system, we know that if we commit a crime, we'll receive a punish-ment and, if we commit a crime again, the punishment will increase. If we need this incre-mental scale, then surely what it tells us is that punishment doesn't work? It contains the problem; it doesn't solve it. If we don't discover and support the **cause**, we can't prevent or negate the **effect**. The purpose of punishment in the criminal justice system is for deter-rence, rehabilitation, retribution, incapacitation, and reparation. Does punishment alone achieve any of this? No.

If we then take the concept of punishment to the *ultimate extreme*, we could live in one of the 27 American states that has the **death penalty**, where inmates are killed by that state after spending time on death row. However, the very fact that 27 states have the death penalty rather points to the fact that it can't be that much of a deterrent: there are approximately 2500 inmates on death row at any given time.[2] In fact, according to Amnesty International, the states that *do not* have the death penalty have lower homicide rates than those that do, and the *New York Times* reports that 83% of those 23 states without the death penalty have lower murder rates.[3] In essence then, punishment, and the threat of it, does not work as a long-term, effective solution.

When I was at university and we considered the purpose of punishment, a lecturer mooted the concept of what would happen if the UK introduced the **death penalty for people who parked on double yellow lines**. He argued that this would be for the **greater good**. With such a harsh punishment, more lives would be saved thanks to emergency vehicles not being blocked than would be lost by anyone parking on the lines – because who would risk their life to do so? But I bet some people still would.

Some people would take the risk of not getting caught, or they'd think that the law didn't apply to them because they think it's ludicrous, or they'd park there because of what they deemed to be their own emergency. However, if they were **explicitly taught** instead the reasons why they shouldn't park there because, after all, most of us prob-ably think the lines exist just to thwart us and raise cash via Fixed Penalty Notices for local councils, as opposed to being there to support our safety, then it might go further to solving the issue. Surely we want young people to have **better morals**, not compli-ance for compliance's sake?

The 'How To'

How to Use Relational/Restorative Practice in Your Classroom

The following 3 examples are excellent practice and will help you to embed RP.

1. **The Social Discipline Window**

A well-known proponent of RP is **Mark Finnis** and if you are teaching in a school that has a relational behavioural policy, then there is every chance that your SLT have read Finnis's work (2021) and incorporated much of it into policies and corresponding prac- tice. Throughout this book, we have considered how important it is to do things *with* one another, and not *to* one another. This concept is propounded by **Ted Wachtel**, founder of the International Institute for Restorative Practices.

   People in authority can be leaders, or teachers, or the actors that Milgram used in his experiment. It's how we use that authority that makes the difference – are we **authoritative** (doing with) or are we **authoritarian** (doing to)?

   This is common sense. Remember when we looked at emotional intelligence and leader- ship styles, and how we feel when we are led by people who do things to us and not with us? Remember what that leads to? Finnis takes Wachtel's (1999) version of the '**Social Discipline Window**' and uses it to demonstrate what this looks like in practice – and it's something that you can reflect on and embed in the relational foundation of your class- room; see Figure 4.1.

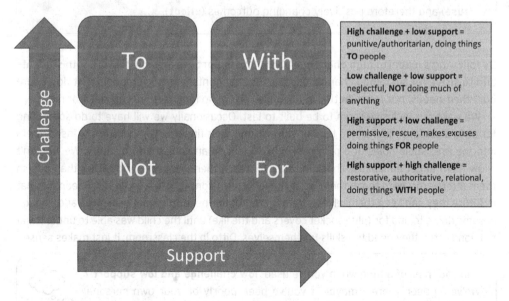

Figure 4.1 The Social Discipline Window Finnis, M. (2021) *Independent Thinking on Restorative Practice*. Carmarthen: Independent Thinking Press.

If we take this further then, and consider how it looks in our classrooms:

High challenge + low support = punitive/authoritarian, doing things **TO** people
What this looks like:
Punitive punishments, not identifying or meeting needs (cause) and therefore having negative outcomes (effects), anxious students whose learning is then affected, feeling unsafe.

Low challenge + low support = neglectful, **NOT** doing much of anything
What this looks like:
Occupy or 'babysit' the students. Watching DVDs, colouring, aimless chatting to pass time, containing the children, passive learners.

High support + low challenge = permissive, rescue, makes excuses, doing things **FOR** people
What this looks like:
Completing tasks for students, low expectations, never removing the scaffold, differentiated tasks but with students pigeonholed in one low ability learning style, little aspiration, passive learners.

High support + high challenge = restorative, authoritative, relational, doing things **WITH** people.
What this looks like:
High expectations, consistency, clear consequences, academic challenge, rigour, routines, trust, adaptive teaching, involved in learning, really knowing our children and young people – including their needs, identifying, supporting and meeting needs (**cause**) and therefore positively changing outcomes (**effect**).

By following a model of **high challenge and high support**, we are able to work with students and to strive for sustained change. Quick fixes that contain kids, or models that don't support their needs, nor teach better behaviours, are of no long-term use in classrooms.

We want our inclusive room to be built to last. Occasionally we will have to do something for or to a student – just as if a toddler were licking their fingers in preparation to insert them into the irresistible holes of a plug socket, we'd leap in and pull them to safety. We wouldn't allow them to get an electric shock in order to 'teach them a lesson'. And rather than punish them afterwards, we'd teach them what the long-term consequence could have been, so that in future they can keep themselves safe. We'd no doubt need to repeat ourselves and engage in some doing to and for (plug socket covers and the like) until the child was able to understand but, long-term, they need the skills for themselves. Ditto in the classroom; it just makes sense.

Can you think of a time when you've used '**low challenge and low support**'? We've all been there – maybe if you've been poorly or your own personal needs for whatever reason are not being met. Those days when we think the school are lucky just to have us there in body if not in spirit, just to prevent them requiring cover or supply staff. We give the young people a doddle of a task and we try to sit clutching our paracetamol, willing them to just get on with it and be quiet.

How did that work out for you?

Are there classes where it has been disastrous? Are there classes where it's OK once in a blue moon? What would it be like if you always worked like that? Can you picture the long-term outcomes?

2. Nonviolent Communication (NVC) and Speaking with the Children

As an integral part of high challenge and high support that we can put into practice, we also need to consider **Marshall Rosenberg** and his work around **Nonviolent Communication**, or NVC (2015). Finnis (2021, p. 72) draws upon the work of Rosenberg, and if you are fortunate enough to be given any training on RP, or, for example, writing Family Support Plans, then no doubt the person training you will also reference him, because a whole host of external agencies recognise the benefits of incorporating this model into conversations that are challenging, or where change is sought.

Rosenberg was a psychologist and he developed NVC in response to trying to **resolve conflict and support relationships**. There are **4 elements** to this model and you can use them in school to speak to students, or indeed any stakeholders, but you can also trial them at home with your own family or partner (I speak from experience!). Rosenberg tells us that these can be used to either express our own feelings and needs, or to empathically speak about those of others. The premise of non-judgement, and avoidance of blame, are central to this. The 4 parts are: **observations**, **feelings**, **needs**, and **requests**, and we must be **explicit** with each of these. We can practically apply this in our classrooms as follows:

NVC 4 Parts	This can be from your point of view or empathically about what has happened to someone else	What to say (Remain calm, clear, and non-blaming. Be clear, be specific and explicit, don't demand, and don't label people)
Observation	What's been seen, for example, a particular behaviour *When I see/when you …*	1) *When you shouted in my face …* 2) *When you didn't turn up to our meeting …* 3) *When I saw you leave your wet towel and dirty pants on the floor …* Be explicit, direct, calm, and do not speak with judgement. Do not use absolutes such as 'always' e.g. *'You're always leaving your wet towels and your filthy pants chucked about the place willy-nilly!'*

NVC 4 Parts	This can be from your point of view or empathically about what has happened to someone else	What to say (Remain calm, clear, and non-blaming. Be clear, be specific and explicit, don't demand, and don't label people)
Feelings (That emotional intelligence again!)	The impact of how this has made someone else or yourself feel *I feel ...* *It leaves me feeling ...* *You felt ...*	(Shouting scenario) 1) *... it left me feeling frightened ...* (Meeting scenario) 2) *... it resulted in me feeling frustrated ...* (Pants scenario) 3) *... it led to my feeling unvalued ...* Avoid labelling, such as '*You're always so lazy you can't deal with your own dirty underwear!*' Avoid saying '*You made me/it makes me*' – try to avoid anything inflammatory/blaming.
Needs	What you or someone else needs or values *What I need is ...* *What I need from you is ...*	(Shouting scenario) 1) *... I need to feel safe ...* (Meeting scenario) 2) *... I need to feel that I can trust you ...* (Pants scenario) 3) *...I need to feel respected ...* Be calm, clear, avoid waffling. Do not therefore say, '*I don't need to feel like a pants-servant for God's sake, when I see them there because you've merrily sauntered on by and just dropped them ...*' etc.
Requests	The actions that you or someone else now need to be taken *Would you be prepared ...* *Would you consider ...* *Are you willing ...*	(Shouting scenario) 1.) *... so I wonder if you'd be willing to work with ELSA to help you manage your anger?* (Meeting scenario) 2.) *... would you be prepared to ring me next time to cancel?* (Pants scenario) 3.) *... are you willing to put your dirty pants in the washing basket?* Avoid demands such as, '*Just put the pants in the bloody basket, it's not rocket science!*'

So, in full, pantsgate reads as:

When I saw you leave your wet towel and dirty pants on the floor, it led to my feeling unvalued. I need to feel respected. Are you willing to put your dirty pants in the washing basket?

This is not a scripted robotic method to speak to one another, but it is an incredibly supportive tool for speaking with (I am trying not to say speaking 'to'!) anyone - especially young people in school - in a manner that is **non-confrontational**, that **allows** people to express their feelings and needs, and to **resolve problems**. It is calm, it's to the point, it's non-blaming, and it encourages empathy.

The conciseness of the language means there is no waffle where meaning is lost. We've all got stuck in the waffle-cycle and we can see the children's eyes glaze over with a 'here they go again' sigh. Avoid this as much as you avoid Fact Tennis. Don't get sucked in, it gets us nowhere. Be **solution-focused** and keep it **clear**.

To summarise using NVC:

Do:

- Use clear, concise language
- Be direct and explicit
- Be honest
- Remain calm with calm body language

Do not:

- Generalise with absolutes (always/never etc)
- Label people (naughty/lazy/bad etc)
- Demand (request instead)
- Blame (you make me/because of you)

Can you imagine now a scenario in which you can use NVC?

Can you consider how **differently** a situation may have turned out if you had used NVC?

Is there someone at home that you can **stealthily** try this on and see what the effect is? I have successfully done so with a teenage daughter, with shockingly good results (I'd previously been rather sceptical!).

Next time you are in class or anywhere in school and a situation arises, be **mindful** of this approach and try it.

3. 'Name It to Tame It' - How to Help Children Manage Emotions

Similarly, neuropsychologist **Dan Seigel**, in his book written with **Tina Bryson**, *The Whole Brain Child*, advocates an approach in which we should **name emotions** (2012). Remember our emotional intelligence here. Seigel suggests that we should try to *use* conflict when it happens – which it is periodically bound to do – to teach relational skills; see other perspectives, empathise, make amends, and so forth.

According to Seigel, we should '**name it to tame it**', essentially meaning that by naming and recognising emotions **explicitly** with our children, we enable them to **own** the emotion, to know that it's OK, and that it will pass. Rather than just telling a child who's worrying that 'it will all be OK', we are instead explicit about how they're feeling and encourage them to be, too. The idea is that eventually this will benefit the child's SEMH because they'll recognise their emotion, recognise what's caused it, and be taught strategies to cope with it. For example:

> Instead of –
>
> *It'll all be OK, just get it over with and it'll be done.*
>
> Try –
>
> *I can **see** that **you're nervous** about giving your talk. **I was so nervous** when I first taught a class that my mouth went completely dry. It **might help** if you look at the back of the room instead of making direct eye contact with the class at first and have your water bottle nearby. I'll be right here supporting you.*

We can see then the links to **Rosenberg's** model: what we've **seen**, how it's made us **feel**, what we **need**, **how** that can be brought about. I would also suggest that it's a useful tool to teach parents and carers to use, as well as to model with our young people. Parenting is ridiculously tough, nobody pushes your buttons quite like the little humans that you've made yourself, but if parents also have some tips on how to speak with children and young people, then so much the merrier.

In essence, we feel better when we are with someone with whom we feel safe (think of **Maslow**, of **consistency**, of **UPR**) and we feel better still when that person is able to verbalise how we feel and teach us to do so, too. Even as adults we can appreciate what it's like if someone, maybe our partner or a friend, gives us meaningless platitudes, whether in response to something we are dreading, or when we are feeling overwhelmed. Just telling us, with the best will in the world, that we've 'got this' or that we're 'strong so don't worry', is no help whatsoever. Worse yet if they dismiss how we are feeling and replace it with some sally of their own instead – and we'll come back to this when we look at **PACE** and empathy shortly.

Call Out the Good!

We'll finish this section with a reminder to ourselves that it is of course just as important that we call out the good that we see. Be as direct about this and how it makes us feel, as we are about the more challenging aspects of classroom life.

Use Rosenberg's model to be explicit about positives – say how they make us feel, say what we need, put forward a request for more!

When I see you collaborating with Sam like that and helping him to work out that equation, it makes me feel so happy. I need to feel like that more often on a Friday afternoon! Would you be willing to collaborate with others in the class who are finding it a bit trickier?

Sometimes it's good to flip things around and adapt – adapting, after all, is what it's all about! And finally, on this point and with all this talk of 'with' and 'to', when you're having a conversation with a child, instead of saying (as we all do), 'I'm talking to you!' to focus them, why not try, 'I'm talking *with* you, I'm not talking *to* you'.

Be explicit, explain why you're emphasising *with*. Inclusion is about feeling included and feeling that sense of belonging.

In fact, why not go full Rosenberg and call it as you feel it: **I notice you rolling your eyes at Tommy whilst I'm talking with you. It leaves me feeling sad. I need to feel that we're discussing this together. Would you be willing to listen?**

PART 3: RELATIONAL (OR RESTORATIVE) PRACTICE

Takeaways

- RP is about the culture we create in our classrooms, our **very own classroom culture**.
- RP is **not** therefore a behaviour management system, and we need to recognise that punitive approaches have no long-term benefit for anyone.
- We can embed RP into our relational foundation, ensuring that there is **high challenge and high support**, being mindful of and drawing from **Finnis'** adaption of the social discipline window to support us in doing so. It will enable us to adapt our teaching.
- We must be mindful of how we support with incidents and how we speak with young people. We can use both **Rosenberg's** (NVC) and **Seigel's** (Name It to Tame It) models to help us to do so.
- Consistency is key.
- Be mindful of the **cause** (seeking it, finding it, supporting it) to positively influence the **effect**.

Part 4

PACE: Playfulness, Acceptance, Curiosity and Empathy

I'll be honest, this for me is the crux of relational approaches. I love a bit of PACE. I'll also be completely transparent and say that when this was first introduced to me as an explicit concept several years ago, I initially thought it all sounded a bit obvious. Maybe, due to the fact that I was working within an Alternative Provision (AP) at the time, this was because we were all doing it implicitly to some extent. But I think that, on reflection, it's the exact same as with so much training that we get – unless we are explicit and we are mindful of exactly what we are doing and why, and correspondingly mindful of the impact it's having, then we'll never reach full potential.

When I re-joined a mainstream environment within the same local authority, I was incredibly surprised that nobody at that point had heard of PACE. However, the headteacher of the AP I had worked in began to roll it out across the city as a concept through training, and if you now google PACE you'll see that other areas have done the same. It should be noted that, as with RP, PACE is long-term and it's an approach. You cannot 'PACE someone'. A teacher once said to me, in relation to a child with significant needs, that they had 'used PACE once and it didn't work'. You'll see exactly why this was when you read on (although doubtless you can already guess!).

Try searching for **PACE** online – you'll get plenty of hits and practical advice from lots of different sources.

Look at some relational (or behavioural) policies for schools in different local authorities – some of these will also include PACE. What differences in **language** can you spot between those that do and those that don't promote explicit RP?

Internet searches for local authorities and RP will also yield results that you can read and place within the context of this chapter. Have a look at how different people and places try and adapt approaches.

How About PACE in Schools?

PACE was first introduced by **Dan Hughes**, a psychologist whose work has included looking at **attachment disorders** and **trauma**. PACE was initially developed as a model for family therapy and foster carers to use with children and young people, but over the past few years it has been increasingly taken up as a relational approach to supporting young people via strong relationships that are built in classrooms and schools. PACE is **holistic** and it's about the whole child, and it's about all children. Over the years, PACE has started being used in educational settings because, of course, educational settings are attended by the very people – children – that it was initially developed for.

As an explicit approach, PACE ties together all the **relational threads** that we have examined thus far. It enables us to build relationships, to support young people who are barely on the first rung of Maslow's ladder, to reach the child who presents as the very definition of being in trauma recovery, or who has never been able to form healthy attachments to trusted adults. It helps us to **connect** with young people – all young people, whether they have had ACEs or not and whether they have SEND or not – but especially those who do have needs, or those who have experienced things that we all wish children never did.

You may have heard the term '**connection before correction**'. This connection can be long-term, for example, once you've built a relationship you then stand a more successful chance of teaching better behaviours to a child. Or, it can be short-term (saying a cheery 'good morning' to connect before you make the request to take the Airpod out; better still if you use a touch of **Rosenberg** to frame that request). Either way, we know by now that we must build connections with young people if we hope to succeed, and PACE supports us in doing so.

The 'How To'

How to Create PACE in Your Classroom

PACE is an approach that is all about strengthening connections, so let's have a look at each aspect of it.

1) **Playfulness**

> Perhaps we associate *playfulness* more with primary key stages than with secondary, but it's just as important across all stages of education. It can be broken down into two parts, playful attitudes and playful resources, the second of which we'll be looking at in Chapter 5 as a component of adaptive teaching in terms of lesson planning and resourcing.

- 'Playful' is exactly as it sounds. Some of the children that we teach will not have fun with their caregivers outside of school. Some will have lost all **sense of joy**.
- Playful does not mean being sarcastic, ever, but – once you've connected with a child and once you really know the child – you can be playful.
- As with **Nurture**, we take nothing for granted about the child or young person and we ensure that we are consistent so that children feel safe.
- We use **UPR** and we show that we enjoy being with and working with the children.
- Laugh together, be joyful. If mistakes are made, be mindfully caring and use **light tones** as opposed to harsh.
- Use your learning around emotions (**Rosenberg**, **Seigel**, and **Goleman**) to ensure that you don't belittle how children are feeling, and read the room, adapting to it, but ensuring that you have fun. This can also help to **de-escalate** situations where appropriate – we're all sensible adults here, we know what appropriate looks like – and you can use non-verbal cues, too.

- Think about how your face looks, think about how you're using your face. Use your **voice** effectively, don't talk in a monotone, speak as though you're telling a story, be engaging.
- To some teachers, this comes naturally. If that's you, you'll think it sounds obvious. However, go out and about around your school and I guarantee that you'll be surprised by how incredibly lacking in playfulness some staff are.
- You may be reading this and recognising that you yourself are lacking in the playful department. It might be that you're too scared to employ playfulness in case it equates to poor behaviour, but remember: **high challenge, high support**. You can still be firm and you can rein a situation back in with a variety of techniques (facial expression, tone, raised hand, etc), but always counteract this when appropriate with the playful. If we are never playful then the students don't take so much notice anyway when we pull out the displeased big-guns. If we are playful and we pull out the displeasure when necessary, then they know we mean business.

2) **Acceptance**

> We all want to be **accepted** as human beings, for who we are. This is as true for children and young people as it is for adults. Sometimes, we might feel less worthy of acceptance and, as teachers, we must work hard to instil that sense of self-worth.

- As it says on the tin: accept who the child is and who the child is not. This does not mean that we don't hold high expectations for them, or that we accept unsafe behaviours.
- Remember again, **high challenge/high support**. We have to ensure children feel safe in our classrooms.
 - We have to use **UPR** - show the child that we are **consistent**, we will not be turning our backs on them, and that whatever they've come to us with or from, we will still treat them positively and with respect.
- Do not judge the child; blaming only leads to shaming. Treat them with **unconditional kindness**. This includes when they tell us to f*** off every time we see them. It may take years to build a relationship with that child, but consistency is key.
- It's important (as parents are often told) to separate the child from their behaviour, so that we do not judge the child as 'being' the sum of their behaviour. We accept the child, we do not have to accept poor behaviour. If we never accept the child, then how does that make them feel? This is like the continual ejector seat: you're not good enough, get away from me, I don't accept you or value you. This only breeds resentment and poor outcomes. Instead, use Rosenberg's model of NVC to respond to being told to f*** off, and look deeper into the need (**cause**) that is resulting in the behaviour (**effect**).
- Remain a **readily available and trustworthy adult**, and this may eventually result in your being that child's trusted adult, and subsequently being the one who makes all the

difference for them. We know from those **cyclic ACEs** that, sometimes, we are making a difference to the future generations of that child too: a true privilege and a *hugely impactful* difference.

3) **Curiosity**

> How often do you find yourself feeling **curious** about a child? How often do you get the chance to find out what really makes them tick? It's so important as a core part of our teacher-student **connection**. We all want people to have some level of interest in us as a fellow human being.

- Be **curious** about the child or young person. Really get to know them. Find out their likes and dislikes and remember as many as you can.
- When you see them around the building, ask after their favourite team, or how their dance competition went, or whether they managed to watch the movie they wanted to see.
- Use their **interests** to tap into and plan resources around these, find out what makes them tick.
- Help the child to feel valued, and as though they're worth getting to know. They may well be resistant for some time - years even - but because we are being **unconditional** with our **positive regard**, be consistent. Do not give up.

- Think about the **cause and effect**. What has caused the child to not enjoy something, or react badly to one thing or very positively to another.
- Be curious about their needs and ask for **external support** in finding out about them and how to meet them.
- Speak with the student about how you can meet their needs. There is little point, as all who've worked with children know, in asking 'why have you done that?' They won't know, or they won't be able to articulate it, so don't bother asking. Instead, use your **emotional intelligence** and link possible emotions to behaviours. You can do this explicitly, as per **Seigel**.
- When you have time ('Have time?!' I hear you cry!), find the child **outside of** your usual learning time with them. Go and see them briefly to say how well they'd done with something, or to check in on them and ask how they are.
- When I taught in the AP, and especially when behind an initially closed door, myself and other staff became incredibly adept at basically having **conversations with ourselves**. This took a lot of getting used to at first - it was very different to a mainstream class-room. Some of us have encountered similar when teaching online during the pandemic, particularly when cameras and mics are off or not working. However, jabbering away to oneself, voicing questions and queries that aren't being pinpointed at a child - or done to them - can sometimes open doors and encourage responses. (*'I wonder why ...' 'do you think ... because I suppose it might be' 'maybe you're finding it tricky to ... or am I wrong? I often am!' and so on.*)

4) Empathy

> **Empathy** is a key player in our emotional intelligence – we know this from look-ing at the work of Daniel Goleman in Part 1 of this chapter. Empathy plays a massive part in all meaningful connections that we make as human beings.

- Empathy is **absolutely central** to everything we do in education, *for all stakeholders*.
- Really listening, really feeling, really appreciating. It can be deeply irritating when you try to have a conversation with someone and you can see them bursting to interrupt (because they're not listening, they're just thinking about what they want to say next). But just as we want to be listened to, so do those around us. This is core to **inclusion**.
- You may well have watched the **Brené Brown** video clip about empathy. If not, please, please do. It's short, sweet, and has a hard-hitting impact if we really listen (RSA 2013). Brown discusses **true empathy** and what that looks like. It goes beyond putting our-selves in the proverbial shoes of another, and looks at how real empathy is an **uncom-fortable sensation**. It's when we take on a little of what someone else is feeling, and that's not pleasant. How many of us can say we truly empathise and take on some of what a student has felt or been through? Or of how their needs affect them? Especially if they're a student who's recently bitten us so hard on our forearm that they've left imprints deep enough to take a forensic mould from.

   Brown also mentions that true empathy **never** begins with 'at least'. This has really stayed with me in the years since I first watched the clip. I remember a friend of mine who was estranged from his father, telling me that 'at least' mine hadn't wilfully left me, because he'd died. It was cold comfort. People look for silver linings because they want to make us feel better, but what's really better all round is to simply *listen*, without judgment, and to use our non-verbal empathy, our facial expressions, our tones, and to just be there for someone.

   For the children and young people in your classroom, show compassion, show empa-thy, and show care, whatever their need or circumstance.

So, PACE enables us to *connect* with young people and to build a sense of **belonging and community** in which they feel safe. Because we are consistent in our approaches, because we don't disappear or actually f*** off when instructed to do so, they know that we are always there to support; we are worthy of their trust. Even if they don't recognise this, or they don't or can't express their appreciation of it, we are there. You are there.

   It's not easy, **so bloody well done**.

Think back to the last time you **truly empathised** with someone. It could be anyone; a story on the news, an image in a paper, a friend, a natural disaster somewhere. How did it make you **feel** when you took on a little of that per-son's suffering?

Can you think of a time when you truly empathised **with a child** at school and their situation?

Are there young people you can think of now whom you **completely accept**, warts and all? Does empathising help us to do so? Are there some children for whom you could make more of an effort to do so?

We're busy, stopping to take a minute can be hard, but it can also make all the difference to our approaches and the authenticity of them.

PART 4: PACE

Takeaways

- PACE gathers each of our 4 relational pedagogies together.
- It allows us to **establish** and **grow connections** with children and young people.
- PACE can be just as easily applied to our relationships with the **adults** in school - and our relationships with other adults outside of school.
- PACE naturally opens the door to a **mutual respect** of one another.
- The 'Playfulness' of PACE is excellent for **adaptive teaching** - we'll focus on this in Chapter 6.

A Summary of Chapter 4

The 'How' of Relational Approaches

As we begin to conclude Chapter 4, let's remind ourselves of what we've been up to:

- Relationships are central to *everything*.
- Punitive approaches *do not work*, especially in the **long-term**. Teaching better behaviour does.
- Relational approaches create a **positive culture and ethos**.
- **Emotional intelligence** underpins everything.
- The **6 Principles of Nurture** provide a sound basis for inclusive classrooms.
- **High challenge and high support** = excellent outcomes.
- **NVC** and **Name it To Tame It** help us talk with children and young people in a manner that supports positive outcomes for **everyone**.
- **PACE ties it all together.**

To put this firmly into context before we progress to Chapter 5, let's leave with two examples, **The Cola Bottle** and **Trauma and the Science of Neglect**. Both of these demonstrate why our relational foundation is so important, and both are useful to remember when we are in school and having a tough day ourselves.

EXAMPLE 1: THE COLA BOTTLE

There is a training exercise used by some external agencies that involves sitting in a circle with a brand new, sealed bottle of cola being passed around. The person from the agency names the bottle - let's say Thaibah - and tells us that Thaibah woke up early having been cold all night because the cost of heating has soared through the roof recently and her nan can't afford to put it on. The bottle is given a jolly good shake, and passed along.

The next person has to continue the story. They think on their feet and say that Thaibah finds her uniform on the floor but her skirt is in the washing machine, wet. Nan can't afford the tumble drier so Thaibah has to put her leggings on, which are non-regulation. The cola bottle receives its second sharp shake in a short space of time, and is passed along.

The third person tells us that Thaibah is dyslexic and finds it hard to manage her time effectively. Before she knows it, she's running late and walks out of the house straight into a pile of dog excrement on the pavement.

You can probably see where this is going. Before Thaibah has even made it through the school gate, she's leapt over enough hurdles to infuriate even the most regulated, adult brain. When Thaibah therefore walks into school and the first thing an adult says to her is, 'You're not in correct uniform. Where's your skirt? You need to go to internal exclusion, you're not walking around the building like that all day!', the lid of the cola bottle, that's been building up and fizzing all morning, explodes. Right over the member of staff who corrected her with no consideration to connect with her first. No gauging of mood or reading of non-verbal cues like facial expression or so forth, just straight in with the correction (and the highly questionable but sometimes real practice of kids missing learning due to a uniform mishap).

If you are **relational** in your approach, you'll be **modelling** a pleasant greeting first, using your **emotional intelligence**. You'll be **curious** first about Thaibah's morning. You'll be **empathetic**. When you find out what the issue with the skirt is (the need or cause), you'll be **accepting**, and go to pupil services and find a spare one. If you're the teacher that Thaibah has exploded over, because sometimes we all escalate a situation due to being human just like the kids are, then you'll use **Rosenberg's NVC model** to speak with Thaibah to **resolve** the conflict. Alternatively, you might be a **different face** that comes along, and facilitates that chat between Thaibah and the cola-soaked staff member. You'll be **relational** and therefore, by default, Thaibah's day and her learning experiences that day, will be **better**.

EXAMPLE 2: TRAUMA AND THE SCIENCE OF NEGLECT

We have touched on **trauma recovery** throughout this chapter, and all relational approaches are about being trauma-informed. The work of David Taransaud is key in this area and takes a deeply insightful look at children who have suffered trauma (Taransaud 2011). Taransaud is a psychotherapeutic counsellor who has worked with former child soldiers in Northern Uganda, where he set up an art therapy department in an orphanage, and so has more experience of the impacts of childhood trauma than the absolute vast majority of us working in education in the UK (and he is subsequently worth listening to!).

Taransaud identifies two opposing 'selves' to the traumatised child. The '**omnipotent self**' (that which protects the child) and the '**vulnerable self**' (that which is wounded). The omnipotent self is what we see played out in acts of, for example, aggression at school, and it seeks to protect the vulnerable aspects of the young person that have been so hurt and neglected. The vulnerable self is relationship-seeking, but it's rarer that we see this side unless we have been patient, employing principles of **Nurture**, and adopting a **PACE** approach. In his work, Taransaud details some excellent activities that can be used with traumatised young people and these are certainly worth employing if you are in the position to do so. Even if you are not in a position in school to organise interventions involving them, then you can certainly employ aspects in your classroom, such as using stories, films, images, music, and masks (Taransaud 2011). I would highly recommend that you do.

In terms of the science of neglect, we know by this stage of the chapter that we should make **no assumptions** about what has or has not happened to the children and young people who enter our classrooms. We should employ **PACE**, get to know them, seek support from our **SENDCO** where needed, and treat the children with **UPR**, consistently. What it's also worth doing is bearing in mind the science of neglect. For those of us who are less keen on the language of emotions, and who prefer a little science, then knowing some of this can support our ability to empathise with the child's needs.

According to **Harvard University**, and myriad other reputable scientific studies, the brains of children who have experienced neglect, develop differently to those of their peers who have experienced healthy attachments in infancy and childhood, thereby **increasing the risk** of cognitive, emotional, attentional, and behavioural needs.[4] The development of the brain is also *physically* affected (Perry 2002). In CT scans carried out on children who have been neglected, or have not received adequate interaction with their caregivers, then areas of their brains were shown to not only be smaller, but even **quiescent** - essentially, dormant. The frontal lobe can present as **smaller**, developing **slowly**, and this is the area responsible for problem-solving, memory, language, impulse control, behaviour, emotional expression, and so on.

If we think back then to the **Still Face Experiment**, Serve and Return, and so forth that we examined in the previous chapter, it paints a concerning picture, and one that should fill us with **empathy** for those young people with whom we work.

The **positive news** here is that you, we, us as teachers, can and do make the difference every day to these children. However hard it can be, and however much we may silently rage, our passion keeps driving us. Stop for a moment and be mindful of this. Don't just nod, or sigh, or roll your eyes at the fabled 'difference'. For once, take a **moment of appreciation** here for yourself because, actually, we teachers are pretty damned incredible. The pressures of what happens outside of our classrooms before we even get in them, let alone inspections, observations, or appraisals, are immense. But we face it, head on, nevertheless. We come back day after day, we dust ourselves off and we try again. And, very often – probably more so than we ever realise – *we succeed*. Somewhere out there, as you sit reading this, there will be children, young people, and adults who remember you. Who remember that you were the one who supported them, who enabled change, who made things *better*.

COMING UP NEXT

- Now that we know how to 'reach the kids before we can teach the kids', **Chapter 5** is going to examine two clear evidence-based approaches to ensure high quality, adaptive teaching (**Rosenshine's Principles of Instruction** and the **EEF's SEND in Mainstream Schools Guidance Report**), with **practical ideas** for adaptive teaching in your inclusive classroom.

Out of the Mouths of Staff

My most testing – and most rewarding – teaching experience to date was a year when I had a small group of Yr11 lads who were pulled out of mainstream lessons because of behaviour. It took me months of persistent, consistent, sheer hard graft until they'd trust me. I refused to ever have them removed from learning; they'd already reached SLT's last chance saloon. Every night I went home and racked my brain for strategies. I used PACE and relational approaches (including one lesson where we sat in a little circle and talked through *Romeo & Juliet* whilst I sorted out the wadded stuffing inside one boy's jacket because his mum had put it through the wash). I had high expectations for the lads but was realistic too – that lesson was a success, and my nurturing approach with the jacket, plus accepting how much it bothered a boy who displayed OCD behaviours due to his needs, worked well at building trust.

They all sat their GCSE English and got grade 2s and above. Given that they sometimes came to me direct from police custody, I took this as a massive success. I had a real soft spot for them, despite the fact that there would be lessons where they stalked the room, stank of weed, farted, screamed, swore, got on furniture or fought. I accepted why they behaved that way whilst also teaching better behaviours. I often think of them and hope they're doing ok in life! I'd like to imagine that, occasionally, they remember me too.

English Teacher, Secondary

When I first went into teaching I remember a young girl whose brother had passed away. Her brother was older and had left the school before my time. I checked in discreetly with the girl, and told her how deeply sorry I was to hear about her brother, following that up with regular check-ins external of the school support in place. She went on to have some SEMH challenges later in her education but she was only ever pleasant and mild-mannered with me. I think emotional support and acknowledgement for children is crucial. It can make or break their school experience. She went onto become a primary school teacher and told me that her own experiences in school, both positive and negative, inspired her choice.

Class Teacher, Primary

I once worked for a headteacher who literally clicked their fingers in the direction that they wanted you to go. You would be ordered about, sent to different rooms to complete different tasks, often not your 'own', and were sometimes actively told that you could not speak to other adults. It was pure autocracy and she lacked any form of emotional intelligence. Staff were miserable and had no respect for her whatsoever.

In comparison, I then worked in a Pupil Referral Unit. Staff were under immense pressure but SLT ensured that, for example, we could take one personal day per term off work. You could go Christmas shopping for example without your own kids hanging off you. Emails were not allowed to be sent unless within working hours, cut off at 6pm, which meant that people who wanted to write them in the evening could, because they had time could do so, but they'd schedule send for the following working morning, or send them direct from drafts.

The working environment was far more challenging, these were children who'd been excluded from mainstream, but SLT led from a perspective of emotional intelligence. Staff were therefore happier, wellbeing was better, students subsequently thrived, and staff absence was low. It just goes to show the difference that winning hearts and minds can make.

Primary Specialist

I worked with one family to support a child's needs and all it took to make the difference to the child's heightened behaviour in school, was for dad to get some toast going in the morning and to chat to the lad before school, for the child's uniform to be ready, and for the family to sit and eat together in the evening, discussing their days. It's rarely this easy but sometimes it really is! We should never assume families function as we 'expect' them to, and sometimes parents can't see the woods for the trees.

SENDCO, Primary

> We once had a child in class who would
> happily give the little girl next to him a wallop with his ruler
> if he was feeling frustrated. Initially, we were using punitive measures
> and, of course, the little girl's parents were furious about what was
> happening so they were requesting a 'punishment' for him. Eventually, we could
> see that punitive responses were having no effect because he just didn't understand
> why he shouldn't do this. Even changing the seating plan hadn't worked. So, we
> changed tack. We explained to both of the children's parents separately what we
> were doing and, when we'd gone through the plan and listened carefully to their views
> and found them to be understanding, we moved forwards with it. We challenged his
> behaviour but we put high support in place. This took the form of ELSA support for emotional
> regulation and we held restorative conversations between the children rather than punishing
> the boy. We had to try and forget our own assumptions that we all know how to
> behave – we just don't – and it was only through careful strategies that he realised
> and was taught both why he shouldn't hit his companion but also how that made
> her feel and how he could manage his frustrations instead. It was after this that
> I realised how important teaching better behaviour is than
> punishing bad behaviour.
>
> *Class Teacher, Primary*

Notes

1 Available at: https://endcorporalpunishment.org/reports-on-every-state-and-territory /uk/#:~:text=prohibition%20in%20law.-,Schools,in%20Northern%20Ireland%20in %202003.
2 https://deathpenaltyinfo.org/death-row/overview
3 https://humanrights.brightblue.org.uk/blog-1/2016/4/22/does-the-death-penalty-deter -crime#:~:text=A%20number%20of%20studies%20have,states%20with%20the %20death%20penalty.
4 Available at: https://developingchild.harvard.edu/science/deep-dives/neglect/#:~:text =Studies%20on%20children%20in%20a,%2C%20cognitive%2C%20and%20behav- ioral%20disorders.

References

Applying Nurture as a Whole-School Approach. (2017). Available at: https://education.gov.scot/ improvement/documents/inc55applyingnurturingapproaches120617.pdf

Babcock, L.D.P. (2018). *Toolkit of Evidence Based Interventions to Promote Inclusion of Children with SEMH Needs.* Available at: https://www.semanticscholar.org/paper/Toolkit-of-evidence-based -interventions-to-promote/fdb1f9a612320af27511d06246b1e61b7b8ad959

Ellis, P. (n.d.). Cambridge Assessment International Education. *Getting Started with Reflective Practice.* Available at: https://www.cambridge-community.org.uk/professional-development/gswrp/index. html

Finnis, M. (2021). *Independent Thinking on Restorative Practice.* Carmarthen: Independent Thinking Press. (See also: https://l30relationalsystems.co.uk/school-services/)

Goleman, D. (2011). *Working with Emotional Intelligence.* New York: Bantam Books.

Harrison, M.E., Norris, M.L., Obeid, N., Fu, M., Weinstangel, H., and Sampson, M. (2015, February). Systematic Review of the Effects of Family Meal Frequency on Psychosocial Outcomes in Youth. *Can Fam Physician*, 61(2), e96–106. PMID: 25676655; PMCID: PMC4325878

Ofsted. (2011). *Supporting Children with Challenging Behaviour Through a Nurture Group Approach.* Available at: https://www.gov.uk/government/publications/supporting-children-with-challenging -behaviour

Oxford English Dictionary. (2016). https://en.oxforddictionaries.com/definition/nurture.

Perry, Bruce. (2002). Childhood Experience and the Expression of Genetic Potential: What Childhood Neglect Tells Us About Nature and Nurture. *Brain and Mind*, 3, 79–100. 10.1023/A:1016557824657.

Rosenberg, M. (2015). *Nonviolent Communication: A Language of Life* (3rd ed.). Encinitas: Puddle Dancer Press.

RSA. (2013). *Brené Brown on Empathy* [online video]. Available at: https://www.youtube.com/watch?v =1Evwgu369Jw

RSA. (2021). Inclusive and Nurturing Schools Toolkit. Available at: https://www.thersa.org/reports/ inclusive-nurturing-schools-toolkit

Seigel, D., and Bryson, J. (2012). *The Whole Brain Child: 12 Proven Strategies to Nurture Your Child's Developing Mind*. Robinson.

Taransaud, D. (2011). *You Think I'm Evil*. England: Worth Publishing.

Wachtel, T. (1999, February 16–18). *Restorative Justice in Everyday Life: Beyond the Formal Ritual* [Paper presentation]. Reshaping Australian Institutions Conference: Restorative Justice and Civil Society, The Australian National University, Canberra, Australia. https://www.iirp.edu/eforum -archive/4221-restorative-justice-in-everyday-life-beyond-the-formal-ritual

Why Nurture Matters. Available at: https://www.nurtureuk.org/what-we-do/whole-school-approach -to-nurture/

Chapter Five

Evidence-Based Adaptive Teaching and How to Do It

Now that we have built our relational foundation, reaching as well as teaching the young people in our inclusive classrooms, let's turn our attention to said teaching. Having **adapted our approaches**, how are we going to **adapt our teaching**?

In this chapter, there are 3 parts:

	Chapter 5	A Summary
Part 1	**Evidence-Based Recommendations for Adaptive Teaching**	In Part 1, we'll look at 2 evidence-based approaches for **high-quality teaching**. Firstly, we'll touch on **Rosenshine's 10 Principles of Instruction** (2012) which give clear and concise guidance. Secondly, we'll consider high quality teaching specifically for children with additional needs, by examining the more recent work of the **Education Endowment Foundation (EEF)** and their Guidance Report for SEND in mainstream schools (Education Endowment Foundation 2020).
Part 2	**Practical Ideas for Adaptive Teaching**	Part 2 will give you practical ideas, based around the **5 strategies** advised by the EEF: 1) Flexible grouping; 2) Cognitive and metacognitive strategies; 3) Explicit instruction; 4) Using technology to support pupils with SEND; and 5) Scaffolding.
Part 3	**Using Playfulness (PACE) to adapt planning and resources.**	In Part 3, we're going to look at how to use our understanding of **relational practice** (RP, specifically **PACE**) to adapt our resources and planning for the children and young people in our inclusive classroom. We'll consider both **why** we need to do this (although by now, we know this really!), and **how** to do this. This will include practical, engaging ideas and encouragement to be *creative*! It will also include a look at **experiential learning and stories** which can be an excellent addition to our teaching toolkit for all children and especially those with SEMH needs.

DOI: 10.4324/b23417-6

The Doors of Perception

The key to the door of our inclusive classroom is, as we know, **consistency**. Consistency of relational approach, of high expectation, and of adaptive teaching methods. This key can open the doors between what children know and what they do not know.

Way back when in the introduction of this book, I quoted William Blake:

> If the doors of perception were cleansed everything would appear to man as it is: Infinite.
>
> *(Blake 1975)*

If we forgive Blake for his androcentric expression, then we can acknowledge that, as teachers, we are the **keyholders to those doors**. We are in the unique and privileged position of both parents and society placing children within our care until they are young adults, and we can inspire young people to see that their perceptive abilities are endless. Whether children are going to follow a route of high academia or of vocational studies should not matter nor make a difference, as long as what they are following is right for them and always driven by high expectation. We can help them to open their personal doors to high aspiration and to be the best that they can be, future-ready, with strong self-belief.

If you were, or are, a parent, what would you **expect** from your child's school?

If you had to suggest **3 key things** that you'd expect or want from that school, what would they be?

Are these 3 things readily available in your **own** school? If so, what difference so they make? If not, what difference does their absence make?

To help children open those doors of perception, we must ensure that we meet the needs in our inclusive classroom. This means the needs of children with SEND but also of those children who just find particular aspects of learning, or of specific subjects, quite tricky. As we've established, not every child who finds a subject challenging has additional needs. We all find some things easier or harder to grasp than others. But whatever the reason, as teachers, we must make learning accessible to each young person in our room.

This chapter will detail evidence-based guidance for high quality teaching and, specifically of course, high quality teaching for children with additional needs. Throughout it, we need to be mindful of our foundation of **relational approaches** and remember that adaptive teaching is all about being **responsive**.

The Use of Formative Assessment

If we return to the **ECF's** guidance for adaptive teaching that we examined in Chapter 1, then we saw that it advised making use of *formative assessment*. This means that we are continuously identifying - and supporting the students to also identify - their strengths and weaknesses. This in turn allows us to see where extra help is needed, resulting in our knowing **when** to adapt our teaching. As teachers, we are assessing the students all the time, and this allows us to recognise when we need to respond to support the children's learning, and to remove barriers to learning. Remember our model of **Cause and Effect,** where we unpick the causes so that we can support the effects.

Methods of formative assessment include:

- Diagnostic questions.
- Quizzes - including impromptu, adaptive ones, on the spur of the moment because of what you're identifying in class.
- Taking votes and making polls.
- Writing answers on mini-whiteboards.
- Think, Pair, Share - then feedback orally.
- Ask students to think of and share a common misconception.

*You'll know plenty of these already and the Internet is full of ideas if you're feeling that you need to change yours up a bit. The gist of this is, assess what the children understand and what they do not understand - and then **respond with adaptive teaching**.*

Part 1

Evidence-Based Recommendations for Adaptive Teaching

With our **relational foundation** in place, and our **key of consistency** unlocking the doors, let's return to our **Toolkit** model for building our inclusive classroom, so that we can remind ourselves of what we now need to focus on to adapt our teaching (see Figure 5.1).

What Evidence-Based Advice Do We Have?

There are hundreds of different studies that we could look at, or organisations, or recommendations for teaching children with SEND, but we don't want or need to get bogged down in these.

Obviously, there is no magic bullet in teaching, but there is excellent advice backed up by research and evidence. Subsequently, I've picked **two such models of guidance**, both of which will also give us a helpful context for when we look at practical strategies for adaptive teaching later in this chapter. You don't need to learn these recommendations by heart or follow them in a rigid manner – it's all about *flexible adaptation* – they just make sense. Use them as a holistic approach and as a reminder.

The main guidance that we're going to consider is the more recent work of the **Education Endowment Foundation's (EEF) SEND in Mainstream Schools Guidance Report (2020)**. Firstly, however, we'll briefly turn our attention towards **Rosenshine's Principles of Instruction**, in order to see how the earlier work of Rosenshine provides an excellent basis for high quality teaching, including some of the recent recommendations of the EEF, and also for adaptive teaching per se.

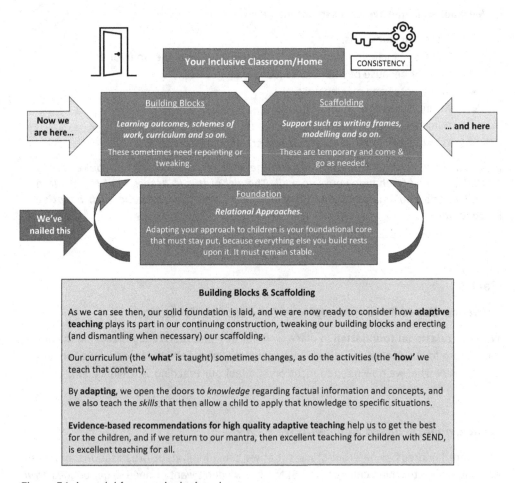

Figure 5.1 A model for your inclusive classroom

Evidence-Based Approach 1

Rosenshine's Principles of Instruction

Barak Rosenshine was a history teacher who eventually stopped teaching in schools in 1963. Not because he'd won the lottery, but because instead he wished to gain his PhD and thereafter taught in universities. It was whilst doing so, that he developed his 'principles of instruction', and in 2012, he published a paper entitled 'Principles of Instruction: Research-Based Strategies that All Teachers Should Know'. (2012)

You will see in the list below how much of what we do in school stems seamlessly from this approach. Remember, excellent high-quality teaching for children with SEND is excellent high-quality teaching for all, and the following provide a solid structure for that high quality teaching:

1. Begin the lesson by reviewing what learning has already taken place.
2. Introduce new material in small, manageable steps.
3. Ask lots of questions and make sure you're asking everyone.
4. Provide modelling and give worked examples.
5. Practise using the new material.
6. Check for understanding frequently and correct errors.
7. Ensure a high success rate among students.
8. Scaffold challenging and tricky tasks.
9. Ensure opportunities for independent practice.
10. Include the students in monthly and weekly reviews.

When we see it like this, laid out explicitly in front of us, it's all pretty logical, isn't it?

Explicitly recapping with the children where the lesson sits in terms of **previous learning**. Moving forwards in **small steps** that are consolidated. Excellent, careful **questioning**. Modelling (including modelling the **non-examples** that we shall see advocated by the EEF). **Practising**. Checking consistently and frequently for understanding or **misconception**. Only moving forwards once we've **ensured** the students have got it. **Scaffolding**. Engaging the children in **independent** work both with, and then without the scaffold. Reviewing frequently.

This is adaptive teaching. This is being responsive to the learning needs in front of us; recognising who gets it, who doesn't, how to help, and where to support. Not moving forwards until **we are sure** that we aren't leaving anyone behind. Adaptive teaching strategies flow from this model of instruction and by applying the 10 principles we **automatically** adapt to need. It just makes sense.

With this model in mind, let's move on to consider the work of the **EEF** – you'll recognise where there are overlaps and links. However, if you'd like to explore Rosenshine further out of an urge to engage in some pedagogical snooping and pondering, and if a podcast is very much up your inclusive street, then Dr Susie Nyman's thoughts are worth tuning into on the SENDCast.[1] Nyman discusses Rosenshine and why his principles are excellent practice for teaching children with SEND in our inclusive classrooms. Do remember, you can dip in and out of these; it's not about sticking rigidly to a set of 'rules', it's about adapting and responding, flexibly.

Are you aware of having moved on in a lesson without **every** single child having 'got it' before you've done so?

If so, **why** is this? Why do we sometimes do this even though we recognise we
are doing so, and we know that we should not?

Is it because we don't think that a child will **ever** 'get it'? Is it because of **time pressures,** or because of the pressure of getting through **content**?

What can you do about this in future? If a child/ren look/s as though they are really
struggling, there's no point just moving on without addressing that gap: it will only lead
to worse. This might be when you need to consider **intervention**. (See the EFF recommendations coming up in our next section.)

Evidence-Based Approach 2

The Education Endowment Foundation's (EEF) SEND in Mainstream Schools Guidance Report

The EEF is a UK-based charity and nationally recognised source of good practice. The aim of the
EEF is to 'break the link between family income and educational achievement', thereby supporting schools to change the lives of some of our most deprived and vulnerable students.[2]

The EEF's guidance report for teaching SEND in mainstream schools was initially produced in 2020 and it gives us **5 clear evidence-based recommendations**.

The 5 recommendations are:

1) **Create a positive and supportive environment for all pupils, without exception;**
2) **Build an on-going, holistic understanding of your pupils and their needs;**
3) **Ensure all pupils have access to high-quality teaching;**
4) **Complement high-quality teaching with carefully selected small-group and one-
   to-one interventions; and**
5) **Work effectively with teaching assistants**.

You can read the report itself for more detail if you wish (rest assured your SENDCO will
have), but the recommendations are laid out in short in the following table.

Depending on your position in school, you won't necessarily play an active part in
developing the vision for whole-school inclusion. However, **we all play our own part** in
contributing to it, building our inclusive classroom to feed into our inclusive school, and
these 5 recommendations are helpful in showing us how we can do so. The 3rd recommendation, 'Ensure all pupils have access to high quality teaching', is where we are
going to focus.

Education Endowment Foundation's (EEF)
SEND in Mainstream Schools Guidance Report
5 Recommendations
(see Pages 8 and 9 of the report to find these)

5 EEF Recommendations *SEND in Mainstream Schools Guidance Report, p. 8–9*	Create a positive and supportive environment for all pupils, without exception.	Build an ongoing, holistic understanding of your pupils and their needs.	Ensure all pupils have access to high-quality teaching.	Complement high-quality teaching with carefully selected small-group and one-to-one interventions.	Work effectively with teaching assistants.
The EEF's descriptors for each recommendation	An inclusive school **removes barriers** to learning and participation, provides an education that is **appropriate** to pupils' needs, and promotes **high standards** and **the fulfilment of potential** for all pupils. Schools should: • promote **positive relationships, active engagement,** and **wellbeing** for all pupils;	Schools should aim to understand individual pupil's learning needs using the **graduated approach** of the 'assess, plan, do, review' approach. • Assessment should **be regular and purposeful** rather than a one-off event, and should seek input from parents and carers as well as the pupil themselves and specialist professionals.	To a great extent, **good teaching for pupils with SEND is good teaching for all.** • Searching for a 'magic bullet' can distract teachers from the **powerful strategies** they often already possess. • The research suggests **a group of teaching strategies that teachers should consider emphasising for pupils with SEND.** Teachers should develop a repertoire of these strategies they can use flexibly in response to the needs of all pupils: – **flexible grouping;**	Small-group and one-to-one interventions can be a powerful tool but must be used **carefully.** Ineffective use of interventions can create a barrier to the inclusion of pupils with SEND. • High-quality teaching should **reduce** the need for extra support, but it is likely that some pupils will require **high quality, structured, targeted** interventions to make progress. • The intensity of intervention (from universal to targeted to specialist) **should increase with need.**	**Effective deployment** of teaching assistants (TAs) is critical. School leaders should pay careful attention to the roles of TAs and ensure they have a positive impact on pupils with SEND. • TAs should **supplement,** not replace, teaching from the classroom teacher. • The EEF's guidance report 'Making Best Use of Teaching Assistants' provides detailed recommendations.

• ensure all pupils can access the **best possible teaching;** and • adopt a **positive and proactive approach to behaviour,** as described in the EEF's Improving Behaviour in Schools guidance report.	• Teachers need to feel **empowered and trusted** to use the information they collect to make a decision about the next steps for teaching that child.	– **cognitive and metacognitive strategies;** – **explicit instruction;** – **using technology to support pupils with SEND; and** – **scaffolding.**	• Interventions should be carefully targeted through **identification and assessment of need.** • Interventions should be applied using the principles of effective implementation described in the EEF's guidance report 'Putting Evidence to Work: A School's Guide to Implementation'.

In Part 2 of this chapter, we are going to zoom in on the 3rd recommendation, **'ensure all pupils have access to high quality teaching'**, but you can find guidance throughout this book regarding each of the 5 recommendations above. If you'd like to look at a table that lays out explicitly whereabouts and in which chapters you can find support linking to each aspect of the EEF's guidance here, then flick along to the **Appendix,** where it's laid out in an at-a-glance table for you, for ease of use.

The 3rd Recommendation of the EEF

The EEF then provides us with an overview of 5 recommendations for teaching children with SEND in mainstream schools. The 3rd recommendation, '**Ensure all pupils have access to high quality teaching**', contains **5 strategies for high-quality teaching** that we can use in our inclusive classroom:

1) Flexible grouping;
2) Cognitive and metacognitive strategies;
3) Explicit instruction;
4) Using technology to support pupils with SEND; and
5) Scaffolding.

We can use these as a clear starting block from which to adapt our teaching so, moving forwards to Part 2, let's look at practical strategies to do so.

PART 1: EVIDENCE-BASED RECOMMENDATIONS FOR ADAPTIVE TEACHING

Takeaways

- Rosenshine gives us 10 principles of instruction that provide a solid basis for excellent practice, and we can then see reflections of these in the EEF's *SEND in Mainstream Schools Guidance Report*.
- In the EEF's report, we can see that the third recommendation, '**Ensure all pupils have access to high-quality teaching**', contains **5 strategies** that we can use in our inclusive classroom. These are:
  1) Flexible grouping;
  2) Cognitive and metacognitive strategies;
  3) Explicit instruction;
  4) Using technology to support pupils with SEND; and
  5) Scaffolding.

- We must **assess** children regularly to recognise where and when to adapt our teaching. As Rosenshine suggests, we must '**check for understanding frequently and correct errors**'.
- We can then adapt our teaching using the recommendations of the EEF for ensuring high quality teaching.

Part 2

Practical Ideas for Adaptive Teaching

In our inclusive classroom, we are aiming to achieve the goals shown in Figure 5.2.

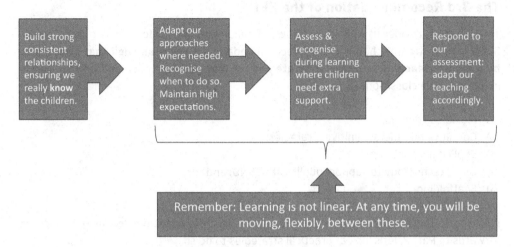

Figure 5.2 The aim of our inclusive classroom

As we saw in Part 1 of this chapter, the EEF give us 5 strategies for **high-quality teaching**, and we can use these to adapt our teaching in-class. Let's look at each, with practical ideas of how you can implement them in your room. These are:

1) Flexible grouping;
2) Cognitive and metacognitive strategies;
3) Explicit instruction;
4) Using technology to support pupils with SEND; and
5) Scaffolding.

Numbers 2 and 5 will have the highest level of detail because they are less self-explanatory than how to, for example, *flexibly group* or *give explicit instruction*. We should bear in mind that adapting our teaching is – as we learnt in Chapter 1 – very different to old-style differentiation, and is more about **responding** to what we see in front of us, rather than creating myriad resources and pigeon-holing students in now-debunked 'learning styles'.

Hopefully, the following will also inspire you to think of further strategies of your own, ways in which to adapt as and when needed, using methods that don't take up the time of old-style differentiation, and which instead show how well you know the young people, and respond to them. You can pick and choose strategies. Some will work for, some won't, others will lead to brilliant ideas that you can share with others.

Flexible Grouping

'Flexible' is key here. This is about grouping children and young people together for a **particular purpose** in learning and, when that's met, they can be **ungrouped**. It's about **not** 'setting' the children in your class – such as putting any learners with a plan for SEND all together on a table. The ECF tells us to be careful using it because of this very point, advising us that 'care should be taken to monitor its impact on engagement and motivation, particularly for low attaining pupils' (Department for Education and Department of Health 2019). When employed with care, it can be a highly supportive strategy. When used to pigeon-hole students, it is not.

Why Flexible Grouping Is Helpful

- You can **change it up** if it's either not working or you see how it can work better. That's adaptation – go for it. Obviously be mindful of needs and plan for/warn of transitions carefully, but this is about getting to know what will work best and then facilitating that.
- Remember Blake's cleansing the doors of perception? When our young people work with others, they can both **implicitly and explicitly** help each other with this. Hearing different opinions, or seeing somebody else approach a task differently, sometimes helps learning 'click' for us.
- It shows the students that you *know them*, you value them, and it encourages stronger social skills. We can therefore also support SEMH needs via mindful, careful, flexible grouping.

How to Use Flexible Grouping

- **Data-driven groups:**

Can you adapt the seating according to who has strengths in what areas? Does each group need a child who can draw, one who can scribe, one who is vocal and so forth? Thinking carefully about what you're trying to **achieve** by grouping children. Use a **combination** of knowing the kids, knowing their data, and knowing the finer mechanics of the class in front of you, to best support learning. Show that you **value** individual skills and knowledge and that you are not pigeon-holing children together.

- **Flexible seating plan:**

For example, can you sit the young people according to numbers 1–6 drawn out of a hat, all the 1s together and so on? Be imaginative. Can there be a sticky-note under their chair to find with their group number on it? Or stuck around the room? Or could each student be handed a question or answer when they enter (simple as 2 + 2) and they have to match up with their corresponding partner via who has the correct answer?

- **Grouped activities:**

For example, **Goldfish Bowl**. This uses children's knowledge and skills. You group the children and they sit in 2 circles, one in the middle of the room surrounded by an outer circle who listen to those in the middle discussing a question or statement you have given them. The children can also pose questions to one another. Group them according to what you want to achieve, based on what you know about them.

- **Know when to end the group:**

It's flexible and a form of scaffolding really; know when it needs to end. Be **needs-led**. Be **responsive**.

> Are your class/es **set** according to 'ability' in your school?
>
> If so, how do you work with that to ensure that teaching is still **adapted** for the individuals in the class?
>
> Do you have a **flexible** seating plan? What grouping do you use now? Or do you have a **consistent** seating plan and then move the children around into groups?
>
> Can children **choose their own groups** once they know enough about their own learning?

Cognitive and Metacognitive Strategies

This is all about children being **self-aware** of their own learning.

Cognitive and metacognitive strategies encourage our students to think about their own learning, and so this links to our being **explicit about learning**. As teachers, we must be explicit about using particular approaches and **why** we are doing so, and children should be explicitly encouraged by us to think about **how** they learn, **why**, **what** they are doing, and so forth. How does it link to a bigger picture? What is the point of it? How about if we try it this way? What if we attempt this instead? The students should be **actively self-aware** of their learning, monitoring it themselves, recognising it, regulating, and motivating themselves.

Why Cognitive and Metacognitive Strategies Are Helpful

- Students are better able to **understand their learning**, to **motivate** themselves, and to be **empowered** to have some control over (and awareness of) their thinking processes.
- **Skilful questioning** is important. Metacognitive skills themselves are oft-heard about when we consider **Bloom's Taxonomy**.[3] This is a hierarchical model, such as Maslow's, only this time it's about steps we must complete in learning. They comprise: **remembering, understanding, applying, analysing, evaluating**, and **creating**. Bloom is sometimes seen as a bit old-skool, but the Taxonomy is still super useful when we are considering the **high order thinking skills** of our students, and our opening of those doors of perception.
- If we consider number 5 in the EEF's list, and 'promoting metacognitive talk in the classroom', then we as teachers are the conductors of this, but the children are absolutely the orchestra – structure it and get them bouncing ideas off each other, developing their **oracy** and their **respectful listening** – and you'll have an incendiary lesson on your hands.

How to Use Cognitive and Metacognitive Strategies

1) **Recommendations**

    In terms of cognitive and metacognitive strategies, the EEF give 7 recommendations in their report (p. 22) which include:

    Explicitly teach pupils metacognitive strategies, including how to **plan**, **monitor**, and **evaluate** their learning.

    Model your own **thinking** to help pupils develop their metacognitive and cognitive skills.

    Set an **appropriate level of challenge** to develop pupils' self-regulation and metacognition.

    Promote and **develop** metacognitive talk in the classroom.

    Explicitly teach pupils how to **organise** and effectively **manage** their learning independently.

    Talk through the learning process, think **out loud**, be explicit about it and have the students do the same. Call them up to the board, or the flip chart, or the mini-white-board, and ask them to **talk through** the problem or the paragraph or the sequence, **explaining their thinking**. Get them to call out possible misconceptions too and **verbalise** how they avoided them.

2) **Questioning**

    For some teachers, this is easy-peasy. For others, it's tough. Questioning can be awkward. We might feel we are putting a child on the spot with questioning but, if our **relational foundation** is solid, then we're on safer ground automatically. When we master questioning, we almost hand over to the children to run with the lesson. If we are a confident practitioner then we can follow where they lead, rounding them back up when required and both igniting an enthusiasm for learning and assessing the students' knowledge and skill, simultaneously.

    When we use questioning, and we use it well, we can **adapt** as we go. We can gauge where the children are at (formative assessment), we can facilitate a whole-class debate, and we can leave the students with very satisfying brain-ache from having thought so hard. Questioning and listening carefully to the responses of others is a clear way to cleanse those doors of perception. Through questioning, we incorporate modelling, practice, small steps - linking clearly then to Rosenshine's principles.

Tips, techniques, and activities for questioning include:

- Ask the students **why** they have a particular **learning objectives** - why is it impor-tant? Is it helpful? How does it **link** to their prior/future learning - or even curriculums in other subject areas? You could give the students different learning objectives to choose from or vote for, justifying their responses considering what they know of their learning and their knowledge or skills-needs. (Note: old-style differentiation often saw teachers writing limiting learning objectives on the board for students. The kind where 'all', 'most', or 'some' students would learn X. This is best avoided and is an example of, albeit unintentional, low expectations.)

- Start with an engaging or **thought-provoking** question, statement, conundrum, or similar. If the children's interest is captured, then it's a strong place to start.
- Use both open and closed questions but **recognise** when each is needed.
- If it's a closed question with a right or wrong answer, and the child is wrong, then use your **emotional intelligence** (Chapter 4). Think about your tone, your body language, your non-verbal empathy - use that RP. Be gentle, guide them around it (such as, 'Ooh I see where you're going there. What if ...'), but do ensure that everyone is clear and there are no misconceptions.
- Give **processing time** where needed. This may mean telling Jannat that you'll return to her in just a mo, to 'bear it in mind and I'll get back to you once I've heard from Annabelle, have a think'.
- **Rephrase/reframe** questions where needed.
- If you're using open questions and you're seeking opinions, never stop and move onto the next child after just one response from the first. For example:

Yousef:	I think stealing is always wrong.
Teacher:	Ok, why? Give me a reason.
Yousef:	Because you're taking something that's not yours.
Teacher:	Yep, absolutely. Why is that wrong though? Can you build on your opinion?
Yousef:	[Remain silent whilst Yousef thinks – do not interrupt, even if it feels awkward, unless it's definitely going nowhere in which case just give a gentle lead.] ... Because, if it's not yours then you haven't paid for it ... and someone else has and that meant they had to work for it. You haven't, you've just taken it.
Teacher:	Excellent. You've paused, thought, and justified that answer; well done. What kind of work do younger people do Yousef, what can we link it to?
Yousef:	I dunno, maybe schoolwork??
Teacher:	Yes! Absolutely! And how do we feel if someone takes our schoolwork or copies it?
Yousef:	Really cross! They're cheats so that's not fair!
Teacher:	Yep, I can empathise with that feeling – although – maybe we need to think about **why** they're cheating? So, Carys, I can see you have your hand up. Can you respond to what Yousef and I have been discussing there?
Carys:	Yeah, I think we do need to look at why someone is cheating or stealing. I don't think stealing is always wrong so I wouldn't always agree with Yousef.
Teacher:	And why is that? Why do you think stealing is not always wrong?
Carys:	Well, you might be poor.
Teacher:	And how does that change your opinion then?
Carys:	Because if a woman had no money for food, she might need to steal some.
Teacher:	Hmm, OK, and what do we need food for? What does it help us do?
Carys:	Stay alive! Live!
Teacher:	So, what if a person who was addicted to a drug had to steal that drug because they couldn't afford it? Does that change things?

And so on – keep going – those perceptive abilities are endless!

3) **Community of Enquiry**

Where possible, sit the children in a circle. You will see the **SEMH benefits** of this activity immediately, and also speaking and listening skills. It goes almost without saying but do reiterate your **high expectations** of respect and then give the students a statement (e.g. the stealing example we have just looked at), or a question (how to best solve a problem), or a conundrum of some form. Anything that links to your intended focus or learning objective. You can check understanding (formative assessment) and adapt wherever needed. The children can also question each other. That **solid relational foundation** that you've laid comes into its own here – if you have created a safe space, then magical things can happen in this kind of inclusive community learning environment.

Carefully choose who is going to begin, and the first child gives their response. The next child has to say whether they agree or disagree with the previous response, being respectful but also demonstrating their thinking skills, by saying **why** they agree or disagree. You facilitate this where necessary, but each student should have a chance to speak. This enables you to **assess**, to **model**, to **address misconceptions** and to progress in small steps.

In this case then, for example, you can lead that discussion to look at why people might have less money than others, you can link in the cost of living, or the cost of electricity, thereby getting those students to think far and wide, adapting your questioning depending on responses, and encouraging empathy and the students supporting one another, bouncing ideas around. Focus on your **why**, **what**, **where**, **who**, **what if**, and **how** questions. Pin these up around the room if you like and refer to them frequently.

4) **Vote With Your Feet**

This is similar to the Community of Enquiry but means the children are up on their feet. Give them a statement, or an equation, or a question, and ask them to move to one side of the room if they agree, another if they disagree, and stay in the middle if they aren't sure.

Once they're in place, you can **facilitate questioning**, asking students to justify their responses, or to bounce off each other's ideas, and even seeing if some students therefore change their mind, or realise a misconception and self-correct, thereby moving to another area of the room. Always ask them to justify their thought process and responses. Encourage and facilitate that metacognitive talk.

5) **Knowledge Organisers**

Students can make these themselves. They can be **dual coded**[4] so that there is verbal and visual information, exchanging words for pictures and so on. The use of words with visuals is helpful for memory and also therefore supports revision. It's better for the students to make these themselves for obvious reasons, but it also means it saves you time.

6) **Cornell Notes**

The Cornell method of note-taking was developed by Walter Pauk. Pauk was a professor at Cornell University in the 1950s and was publicised in his book, *How to Study*

Cue Column	Main Idea
Key words/vocab/terminology Key Questions Prompts	Concise notes – no waffle Paraphrasing/abbreviated/key points only Diagrams/sketches/doodles
Summary 2 or 3 sentences summarising the topic/text/concept/learning	

Figure 5.3 Cornell Notes

Referenced as: Pauk, Walter; Owens, Ross J. Q. (2010). How to Study in College (10 ed.). Boston, MA: Wadsworth.

in College (2010). Such was the success of the Cornell notes method, that you can even buy paper that is specifically printed with the requisite 3 columns on it, ready for use. In school of course, we can hand out standard paper and use it as an excuse for the students to practise their ruler-straight line skills.

To make Cornell notes, you simply have two columns with a summary box or space at the bottom of the page. The first column is the **cue column** (key words, prompts, questions and so forth) and the second column is the **main idea** of what you're study-ing (paraphrased, abbreviated, with sketches/diagrams, concise notes). The **summary** area then requires the student to write a couple of sentences summarising everything. It can be used then for revision or learning. You can cover the **main idea** column and use the **cues** to practise recall of what is in it, for example (see Figure 5.3).

7) **Chunking**

This links very closely to scaffolding. Rosenshine suggests that we present '**new material in small steps**', and the EEF guidance around cognitive and metacognitive strategies, as well as explicit instruction, are intrinsic to this. It makes perfect sense. Learning can be likened to building blocks, or indeed our metaphorical building of our inclusive classroom. If we do not have a solid foundation, then everything else is shaky. By presenting material in small steps, we do not overwhelm children and we are better able ourselves to ensure that our students understand before we move on.

Chunking allows us to build knowledge over time and more complex information can subsequently be accessed and **interleaved** as the child progresses, embedding understanding at each step along the way. Our curriculum should allow our children to **acquire and use** skills, thereby possessing the ability to apply their knowledge to practical situations, such as solving a problem.

Chunking therefore makes sense. It's a logical method of adaptive teaching and we can do it in a variety of ways:

- **Break It Down**

  When you present new material, do not overwhelm the students, it will lead to cognitive overload. Of course, they need to know the bigger picture (for example, writing to persuade), but we need to introduce this step by step. Do not move onto the next step until each is grasped. Some students won't need this as much as others, so you can adapt and change it up for them but remain aware of what's afoot in your classroom.

- **Creative Methods of Instruction**

  Written on sticky notes, or the board, or on a mini-whiteboard, or on a slide. Alternatively, write them in the student's book when you're checking in with them.

- **Repetition**

  Repeat the instructions, ask key students to repeat them back. Ask other students to repeat them to the class, such as, 'I'm getting on a bit, remind me Jude, what are we doing first? Brilliant, has everyone got that? Connor, what did Jude say we're doing first? Humour your old teacher!' Use your **emotional intelligence** and **relational grounding** here.

- **Working Memory**

  If you've ever read an EP report (one from an educational psychologist who has assessed a student), then you may well have read about 'working memory' in one of those. Working memory is all about holding information in our heads. Some children who struggle with this may present therefore as, for example, finding it tricky to hold their knowledge about fractions in their head, at the same time as trying to skilfully multiply two fractions. As well as embedding that knowledge through **repetition** and the **practice** that Rosenshine advocates, we can support a child by both chunking and scaffolding – break the task into small steps, scaffold it using a checklist, or points on sticky notes. Ensuring that they have one instruction at a time, helping them to hold the information themselves.

  Supporting a child's management of their own working memory like this, also teaches them skills for life, so that they can apply these strategies to situations outside of school.

- **Revision**

  There is little doubt that some students find it very hard to revise. Let's face it, revision is boring! The student needs to understand something before they can revise it, and we support this with our adaptive teaching, but then they are left having to memorise huge amounts of work. There's no way around this, it's a fact of our testing methods in schools. However, we can teach students how to revise, how to test ourselves, how to make revision cards and so forth. Techniques such as real mind-mapping, with colour-coding and visuals, can benefit many learners. Do this from as early an age as we are able, so that it embeds.

How do you currently use metacognitive strategies?

How do you think the **social discipline window** (Chapter 4) fits in here? (High/Low Challenge, High/Low Support?)

Explicit Instruction

With explicit instruction, we absolutely do not want or mean the kind of teaching that took place when I was at school - teacher at the front, talking at the class, students expected to just sit, listen, and somehow learn. Instead, this is about being **crystal clear with the children**. It links to Rosenshine's Principles, and essentially it is simple logic.

Why Explicit Instruction Is Helpful

- **Understanding** is checked along the way.
- Any **misconceptions** are dealt with to ensure that students don't proceed under a misapprehension.
- Students can embed **new knowledge** and master **new skills** - thereby applying their knowledge to specific situations accordingly. The EEF (p. 24) recommend using '**non-examples**' with children as opposed to only modelling correct ones, so that they recognise where mistakes are made and can also therefore avoid them in future.

How to Use Explicit Instruction

1) Instructions should be given **clearly**, using **clear language**. Make it **concise**.
2) Instruction should be given in a **logical sequence** and broken into smaller, manageable **chunks**.
3) Verbalise the thinking process - use **clear modelling** - and be clear about **possible misconceptions** (we can see then how this links to cognitive and metacognitive strategies, too).
4) Give plenty of opportunity for **supported practice** with feedback at each step.

> **Where** do you already use explicit instruction?
>
> How can you incorporate it **further**?
>
> Are you always clear about possible **misconceptions**? How do you address or deconstruct these?

Using Technology

These days, there is an entire host of technology at our disposal. Find out what's available in your school, research technology around your subject specialism. In terms of teaching children with SEND, this can be a bit of a **specialist area** around which you'll need more support. It goes rather beyond the obvious tech that we all use in our classrooms and is more about having a specific, supportive impact on learning for children with SEND, and making it accessible.

There may be times when, for example, a child uses **specialist equipment** to support their additional needs and you will need to know how this works, such as an assistive hearing device. You will sometimes have young people in your classes who require specialist seating. Equipment such as this may be funded by the child's family, the school, or the local authority's inclusion team, via an ECHP if a child has one. Or, if relatively inexpensive, then a particular service may fund it, for example, a Speech and Language Therapy Service may fund a voice-output communication aid.

In cases such as these, your SENDCO and your Learning Support Department will contact you directly – and obviously you can approach them – and they will give you specific advice and modelling of how to use the equipment. It's also important to liaise with parents, carers, and obviously – most importantly! – the child themselves. Do not be afraid to do so, be fully inclusive of the child in their learning, value their input, act on it.

There are also various devices in school Learning Support Departments that children can use. Usually, they'll need to have these allocated due to numbers and funding, but Kindles, for example, have some brilliant features on them that make reading much more accessible. Some students will be able to use laptops, others may use assistive reading tools. This can be daunting but, in my experience, it's a bit like kids with the TV remote control and mobile phones; adults can use barely 5 functions on them, kids can probably use them to launch rockets.

Why Technology Is Helpful

- Technology opens doors itself to children and young people these days – specialist programmes, equipment, and so forth are myriad and suited to a **whole host of needs**.
- It provides us with **different methods** of recording work, accessing learning, engaging in learning, the speed of working, the way in which work is presented and processed, understanding written information, improving coordination, finding information, and so forth.

How to Use Technology

1) Your **SENDCO** will be the person who knows what technology a child is entitled to or could benefit from (for secondary school you'll also be thinking about access arrangements for GCSEs).
2) As a year group or department, you may have access to apps, tablets, laptops, PCs, programmes, and interventions that come under this heading. Find out what is available to you – it's a hugely varied area. For example, a child may need a touch-typing intervention as part of their EHCP. This will usually be on a laptop and overseen by a TA or LSA.
3) Your **Learning Support Department** is the place to head if you need some guidance, but in some cases, they'll most likely have already let you know if, for example, a child with an EHCP has it in their plan that they must use a reader pen, or a specific piece of **assistive technology**. Your SENDCO will be able to teach you how to use it but very often the best source of support will be the student. The children are generally

technology whizz kids compared to many adults, having been raised (for better and worse!) on a diet of it.

4) It may be helpful (or even detailed in a plan of support) to print Power Point slides for some children so that they have a copy to refer to, or to read more easily, or to use with the 1:1 adult support, should they have an LSA or a TA.

5) Be mindful of lighting and glare in classrooms - involve children with SEND in where they are most comfortable sitting when using technology.

6) Using visualisers, online quizzes, revision tools, music, virtual reality, and so forth - resourcing using technology - can all be excellent methods of teaching for all children, when used well.

> How **confident** are you to use assistive (or any other) technology?
>
> What is available in your school? Is there a lack of **funding** for technology?
>
> Do you receive **training** in your school on how to get the most and best out of technology in the classroom?

Scaffolding

We know already that our scaffolding is **temporary**. We can pop it up when we need some support, and we can take it down again once we've mastered a skill. What's especially good is if the child recognises when the scaffold is needed, and when it can be removed. (This is a good example of metacognition and self-awareness of learning.)

Why Scaffolding Is Helpful

- Scaffolding gives **structured support** to the building blocks of learning.
- It makes things **manageable** - and it's less daunting.
- It models how young people can manage their own work in future.
- It's temporary and **removable,** which can therefore be **empowering**.
- Know when it's needed, know **when it can go.** Nobody wants scaffolding blocking their view ad infinitum.

How to Use Scaffolding

1) **Writing frames**

   We all know about writing frames, but we do need to make sure that we use them in a manner that's actually helpful. They can be for a whole class. And do remember that the **same children do not always need the same support**. Adapt it according to what they're finding challenging. You can use pre-printed frames that have little clocks on them so that children can see a set time for the task to take. You can use frames that act as checklists for tasks. You can even use frames that have Makaton symbols on them. All of these can be found online to save you time. Do remember that one purpose of adaptive teaching though is to not spend hours making different sheets for each child in the lesson, and never allow a writing frame to limit a child.

Some children will hardly need the scaffold, others can follow what's on the board, some will rely on the scaffold at first. You'll know when to then **adapt** this via your assessment of what's afoot. If you suddenly realise mid-task that Niamh needs more or less support, you can adapt along the way. Be creative. Be responsive.

2) **High quality textbooks**

If we think back to Chapter 1, then the ECF advises that we cut workload by using 'well-designed resources'. A well-written textbook is an excellent resource and by using the kind of sticky notes that have **clear plastic** on one side, it is easy to get the students to annotate and then put these notes in appropriate places to demonstrate their understanding. Alternatively, we can stick them in to show the student which part of the text to focus on, so that they're using the exact same resource as everyone else but in a more accessible way than a student who may be expected and able to use the entire source. Equally, the student may then find, by having access to the entire source, that they can access more of it.

3) **Visuals**

Use images, use visual prompts. These can be on writing frames, slides, checklists, and so on. For students whose literacy is low, then visuals can be both helpful and also inspiring of thought.

4) **Power Point**

You can have a checklist or a frame displayed on a slide. I am always wary of death-by-Power-Point for teaching when it's used to 'deliver at' passive learners for each and every lesson, but it is of course an excellent teaching tool when used efficiently and not endlessly.

5) **Sticky notes**

The joy of the sticky note! Super quick, easy to use, and an immediate provider of live feedback. You can use these to write prompts for children, such as 'rhetorical next!' if using SPAMROD for example, or 'So, in conclusion ...', or even the formula for finding the radius of a circle. You can doodle something on a sticky note, or demonstrate handwriting, or you can use sticky notes that are the colour of the paper that a student who is dyslexic may find easier to read from. You can hide sticky notes (more of this in our Playfulness adaptations), and you can scaffold to your heart's content with them, as can the students, for example, writing a sentence or a paragraph on each (size of your notes dependent) to build up to a bigger piece.

6) **Modelling answers**

Think back again to the EEF report and to Rosenshine. Model on the board, model a maths answer using a visualiser, ask a child to model something to the class. It makes perfect sense to show the students what something needs to look like, or indeed what something should not look like. We must be explicit. Model answers **and** misconceptions – think back to cognitive and metacognitive strategies.

7) **Sentence starters**

Give prompts to the students who need them. These can be written or verbal. Pop them on a sticky note, get them started. Provide random connectives, or symbols that might be needed, and ask the student to choose appropriately.

8) **Clues**

Provide clues of what to look for. Hint, infer, suggest. Point out possible clues around the room, or on the board, or further back in their books. Link to prior learning, or learning yet to come.

9) **Equipment**

You can also scaffold what equipment a child might need for a lesson and for upcoming lessons. Give advance notice, support the child in organising their equipment, liaise with parents, if and when needed. When speaking about this with the child, you can note down equipment but also focus on teaching them why they need it – question them just as you would about academic outcomes. Link the use of equipment to previous learning and lessons, ask how it might also help in other lessons, make cross-curricular links between learning. Ask the students what equipment might you use in maths and also geography, for example.

10) **Pre-learning vocab**

This is something that plenty of teachers do frequently but it is worth noting. Giving out trickier vocab in advance can be used to excellent effect. Glossaries can be stuck into books or written in by students. Vocab can be sent home, or given to an adult 1:1, or passed to an intervention teacher.

Have vocab around the room, use visuals where necessary. Refer to the vocab explicitly. Refer to it throughout lessons. The EEF suggest using the Frayer Model (1969) for learning vocab; see Figure 5.4.

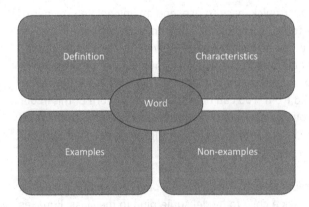

Figure 5.4 The Frayer Model

Referenced as: Frayer, D., Frederick, W.C., and Klausmeier, H.J. (1969). A Schema for Testing the Level of Cognitive Mastery. Madison: WI: Wisconsin Center for Education Research.

This can be used then for any vocab or even shapes and formulas. The child can also use visuals and images if necessary. It breaks down the word, makes links, and means that we give the non-examples that the EEF suggest, thereby ensuring there are no misconceptions.

Remember, once a child doesn't need the scaffold, remove it. They may need it back again at some point, but they shouldn't become reliant on them. Rosenshine makes clear the need for **independent practice**. Once a concept has been grasped, take down that scaffold. **And be creative**!

How **effectively** do you use scaffolding?

Which **methods** do you use?

Are there times when you've had to **reintroduce** it and if so, how did you try to ensure that this time the learning was **embedded**?

Can you think of a time when you could have used it **very** effectively? What did that look like?

OTHER ADAPTATIONS

There will be some adaptations you'll need to make, such as providing coloured paper for children who are dyslexic, or using larger fonts for some young people, or creating accessible entry to the classroom. This will be detailed in the **plans** for those children and your SENDCO will make you aware. These are things you can do in advance and that you'll be advised to do - they are not the same as adapting teaching based on your knowledge of the pupils' understanding. They are still important of course, but they don't need to be covered in detail here.

The other thing you'll need to adapt - some of which may be written into plans but all of which is worth bearing in mind - is the **environment** of your inclusive classroom.

For example:

Lighting - be aware of glare and reflection.
Setting up **'stations'** around the room ('imagination station', 'regulation station' and so on).
Placement of screens and devices.
Seating - can it be in a circle? Can it be easily moved?
Displays - framing work, as opposed to just sticking it up, to show that you value it. Or having an 'In the Frame' picture frame, where a really fab piece of work is displayed weekly/monthly.
Equipment - visual labels so students can identify it (or clear boxes that they can see through to save you the hassle of labels), mini-whiteboards close at hand, ditto for sticky notes.

Metacognitive questions pinned up around the room – how, what, why, when, what if, how about etc.

Not too busy in terms of clutter or colour, or general mess – be mindful of **sensory overload.**

PART 2: PRACTICAL IDEAS FOR ADAPTIVE TEACHING

Takeaways

- We can adapt our teaching by using the EEF's 5 strategies for high quality teaching:

  Flexible grouping;
  Cognitive and metacognitive strategies;
  Explicit instruction;
  Using technology to support pupils with SEND; and
  Scaffolding.

- By using these 5 strategies and being mindful of Rosenshine, we are able to adapt our teaching by being **responsive** and employing a host of **practical ideas** to support learning.

Part 3

Using Playfulness (PACE) to Adapt Planning and Resources

Having examined the guidance of the EEF in terms of teaching children with SEND (and remembering that high-quality teaching for those children is high-quality teaching for all children), we are now going to look at practical ideas for adapting our teaching using **Playfulness** – part of the **PACE** (Playfulness, Acceptance, Curiosity and Empathy) approach that we examined in Chapter 4.

Throughout Part 3 of this chapter, we must continue to be mindful of the **EEF's 5 strategies** for high-quality teaching that we focused on in Part 2. You will see how the more playful, experiential ideas in this chapter link to them.

- Do you try to incorporate **playful planning** in your lessons? Do you think this depends more on whether you're a primary sector teacher?
- If you are a senior sector teacher, does your department plan together? To what extent is Power Point used? Do you feel **comfortable** teaching without it?

- Is your adaptive teaching 'ticked off' via Power Point? For example, a starter that includes an extra 'challenge'? Might this be limiting? If so, how? If not, why not?
- Do you feel under pressure to keep learning less playful in order to prepare students for **testing conditions**? Does getting through **content** ramp up pressure?
- Do you feel as though playful learning can't be done due to behaviour in lessons? If so, how might your RP support this? We can get stuck in a vicious cycle here – take a few risks with playful ideas from this chapter and see what differences it leads to. Remember, for some children, **until we reach them, we can't teach them**.

Why to Adapt Teaching Using Playfulness

In Chapter 4, we examined 4 relational pedagogies with practical advice on how to employ these approaches in your inclusive classroom, thereby embedding that foundation so that all else can flourish upon it. One of those approaches was that of **PACE (Playfulness, Acceptance, Curiosity and Empathy)**, initially developed by Dan Hughes. In this chapter, we are going to focus on the P of PACE, the **Playfulness** element. However, rather than using it as an *approach* as we did in Chapter 4, we are going to use it to adapt our *planning*.

We often think of adaptive teaching as being all about the strategies that we looked at in Part 2, the more traditional elements, such as chunking work, and these are of course crucial in the classroom. However, if we can also **adapt our planning using our RP**, then so much the better.

It's well-known that in Early Years education, children **learn through play** and playful experiences. The further up the school they get however, the less this happens. Out comes the pressure instead, the testing, and, sometimes, the Power Point overkill.

If you search online for 'play' or, for example, 'deep play' (Geertz 1972) you may be as surprised as I was to see the variety of types of play that come up. It transpires that entire philosophies have been written about play. As we grow and become adults, we tend to think of it as something meaningless, frivolous, and as a separate entity to 'real life' or 'work', when in fact, all play links to learning. If we watch small children playing, we see how entirely lost they become in it, emerging at the other end with new understandings, having made links that they previously had not seen, or using skills with a greater level of competence. So it is for adults, and all stages of human development in between.

We know the importance of relational pedagogies in 21st-century teaching and the theories behind these approaches (Chapter 3), and we know therefore that we have children in our classrooms who are not going to respond to coming in and sitting down for hours, ready to learn and to trust. The trust element of this is built via our relational foundation – and this can open the children to learning, but once the doors are opened, we need to engage and inspire those children in such a way that they want to stay. That they begin to see the relevance of learning, that they begin to enjoy learning, and to value it.

It is simple logic that if we have young people in our classroom who are barely even on the first rung of Maslow's hierarchical ladder (Chapter 3), then they are not going to be ready to have learning 'delivered at them'. We need to engage those young people. We need to recognise that even 15-year-olds are still children. And we need to adapt our planning accordingly. As we saw in the EEF's guidance, we need to **'create a positive and supportive environment for all pupils, without exception'** and **'build an ongoing, holistic understanding of your pupils and their needs'**, and subsequently, using PACE to adapt our lessons feeds seamlessly into this guidance.

This chapter then is going to give you practical ideas for adapting lessons and resources using play and, also, **experiential learning**. It would be impractical to suggest that every lesson you teach is adapted in this manner, and it would also be unnecessary and inappropriate for you to do so. However, the following methods are simple, creative, quick to plan, and they are engaging. They inject some fun into learning. Use them when needed, with children who need them – you'll recognise when, just as you recognise when a child needs scaffolding (and when they do not). Have fun with these ideas, share them, add to them, think of your own. Hopefully, you'll enjoy them as much as the kids do!

How to Adapt Teaching Using Playfulness

Practical Ideas

This is all about making learning interactive. Engaging the young people, whatever their age. Be as creative as possible. This is not about spending hours planning – in fact, it shouldn't take you long at all – but it is about using your imagination and seeing everything around you as a possible learning experience, or as being capable of creating a memorable learning experience.

Experiential Learning and the Power of Stories

Experiential learning is excellent for building **inclusive classrooms**, and I find it especially good practice when adapting for young people with SEND. It has fantastic links to the **questioning** that we looked at as part of the EEF's *Cognition and Metacognition* in Part 2 and is an excellent way of making learning relevant to students.

If you've not incorporated it before, then a gentleman called **John Dewey** is generally cited as being a founder of experiential learning (Kolb 1984). Dewey, in 1915, noted a need for **hands-on learning** and advocated that students need to be *active in the learning process* (linking therefore to cognition and metacognition), with children unable to utilise learning outside of the school building, suggesting that they do not see their learning in school as being relevant to their everyday lives, and vice versa. Essentially, experiential learning should enable the students to learn by doing, therefore relating 'theory' to their own practical lives. True experiential learning means getting out there are doing it for yourself, but that's not often practical so, instead, we can tweak things to get the children really involved.

- How often have you heard children question why they need maths when they have a calculator? Or why bother reading a map when they have satnav? Or what's the point of RE if I don't believe in a god/s?
- In fact, many of these questions nowadays boil down to: why bother with (insert relevant learning here) when I have a **phone** to do it for me??

Back when I was a subject leader for RE, I was asked all the time what the point was of studying RE. And it was all well and good to keep reiterating that it's a subject that enables us to learn about people, about how they live, about what's important to others, or how to think about challenging ethical arguments that can affect us all. However, very often, unless children *directly experience something*, it holds little meaning for them theoretically.

Practical Example: The Island

With experiential learning, the doors are opened. One excellent practical example that can be used for children with SEMH needs, and that can easily be adapted for a whole host of curriculum areas, is an activity called **The Island**. This was originally written by a teacher called Sue Phillips and I have returned to it again and again across the past two decades, always with excellent results.

Phillips now delivers on a PGCE course, but when teaching in schools she used to refer to her classroom as a '**Theatre of Learning**'. I was once lucky enough to visit it and was thoroughly inspired. Phillips' pedagogy was entirely based around adaptive teaching, and she has since published a handbook for The Island, demonstrating how it also meets the curriculum, teaching and learning expectations, and pressures that are placed upon us by the inspections-that-shall-not-be-named (Phillips 2013). I've used it with children in both primary schools and Key Stages 3 and 4; it is entirely transferrable. All you need is a little imagination and you're away. There are even social media pages set up for The Island.[5]

Essentially, The Island is told as a **story**. The students become very involved in it, taking ownership of the story and becoming a character within it, using listening skills, empathy, oracy, and a huge number of Bloom's thinking skills. We see then how it also links to the EEF's guidance and the strategies for high-quality teaching. You can build a 'set' in the middle of the room, sit students in a circle, light candles if health and safety allows (batteries if not!), and involve the students fully.

The story involves a cruise ship that crashes onto an island, leaving the passengers stuck, with no chance of rescue. Essentially, they are **back at the start of civilisation**: no phones, no readily available support structures, or rules, or leaders, or devices. No material possessions aside from what is on the ship – **how will they survive**?

This concept of **survival** can be a starting point, but it can be led anywhere, such as:

- How do relationships form? Why are they important?
- Do we need leaders? If so, why? Who will they be? How will we decide on them? (Voting, qualities of leadership, do age and experience matter?)

- What about rules? And what if we don't follow them?
- What about shelter? How will we build it?
- How will we measure angles, or lengths of wood?
- Which materials are available and which are best? Where will we source them from?
- What about community? And belonging?

If we use our imaginations then, the possibilities **are endless**. Just like those perceptive ones that William Blake spoke of. The students empathise to the extent that they can see the relevance of, for example, rules in everyday life. Why we have them, what they contribute to, how to decide on them.

Explicit instruction can be used, **flexible grouping**, Bloom's Taxonomy and **meta-cognition**, reviewing previous learning, small steps, practice, **scaffolding**. As we can see then, this fits into the context of the strategies suggested by the EEF. It slots in seamlessly with Rosenshine's Principles, and it is high-quality, adaptive teaching. The students can sequence the story, retell it, recall, evaluate parts, and so on.

The story can be told over any number of lessons and returned to in future. It is astounding how engrossed the students become. **Diaries** can be written, **formulas**, **maps**, **plans**, **diagrams**, and so on, depending on what learning outcomes you are incorporating. Students could **build mini-islands** or dens and shelters and work out how to do so. The children can compare how this would be done with **technology** as opposed to without and demonstrate it.

'**Story**' as a concept can be used in myriad ways for adaptive teaching. Everyone, no matter what age, enjoys a good story. How could you use one to teach? Experiential learning can be adaptive teaching at its best – all students included and all students *feeling* included, accessing learning, feeling valued, producing good work and demonstrating both skills and knowledge. Give it a go – I am positive you won't regret it.

USING THE ISLAND TO SUPPORT SEMH NEEDS

When I used the story for a weekly intervention that ran for one term for Year 6 students with SEMH needs, the outcomes were wonderful.

I made a '**set**' that is easily packed away in the middle of the room, with logs propped up in a triangle and fairy lights underneath them as our 'campfire' to sit around.

Pieces of driftwood, clothing, sea shells, a wooden anchor – any bits and pieces I could easily source from home were used. The children sat in a circle listening, the sound of waves playing on speakers, as I told the tale each session.

Once the weekly instalment was complete, it was over to the children, with my facilitating the questioning. They began to build a little community. To **listen** to one another, to **think hard**, to **plan**, to **share**, to **construct**, and **evaluate** how to move forwards.

They made **maps to scale**, wrote **diaries**, spoke about **respect** for the elders on the Island and how that could be shown. They decided that **rules** were needed, and **why**. And **what** those would be – and how to deal with it when rules were not followed. They considered why some people might move elsewhere on the Island because they had **different beliefs**, and what they might do on the anniversary of 'landing' on the Island and why that **commemoration** would be important. You can see then that this is also excellent **RP** in the **teaching of SEMH skills**, almost via stealth initially, and then **made explicit**.

The outcomes with Year 6 were just as fantastic to see as when I've used the same activity with Year 7s and GCSE students alike.

Practical Playful Activities

Dip into these, be inspired by them to think of more. These can be used to meet a variety of outcomes. Be creative with them and adapt them to your year group or subject. These will support with engagement, accessibility, and the creating of active learners. Each activity can incorporate parts of the EEF's 5 strategies for high-quality teaching (flexible grouping, cognitive and metacognitive strategies, explicit instruction, technology, and scaffolding), and many give you an opportunity for formative assessment. Remember your **high expectations** – being playful isn't about lowering our expectations. All of the following should be adapted to be appropriately challenging (for example, your questioning skills can turn an activity from 'playful' to 'high order thinking' in a flash).

(Note to the obvious: there may be **health and safety or sensory needs** to consider. You know the children well, so you'll know what may or may not work.)

Pass the Parcel

What can you wrap up? Can you put different things in each layer? Questions, quizzes, directions, facts, riddles, instructions? Can students choose and justify who it's passed to next? Can they guess what's going to be in the middle or evaluate what's in there?

Using Scents in the Classroom

Using smells can be super effective in capturing imagination or thought.

For example, use oranges studded with cloves, cinnamon or nutmeg in spice jars, scented candles and so on to capture 'Christmas'. Students can work in pairs, close their eyes, or wear a blindfold and guess what the scents are representing.

This can be used for different seasons (autumn leaves for example), or subjects (*A Christmas Carol*), for evocative imagery and creative writing. It can be used in science, or DT, or across the curriculum if we are creative.

How could you use it with your class/es?

Jelly Babies

Jelly Babies were called 'Peace Babies' after WW1. The colours of them can also represent diversity and LGBTQIA+.

You can flexibly group students – all yellows in one group, reds in another and so on.

How else can you use them?

Coloured Sand Activity

This activity requires:

Coloured chalk, small bottles or jars, table salt, paper to pour the salt on.

Students use coloured chalk to shade in table salt. Hold the chalk horizontally to do so – it's quite a speedy process. This results in layers of what look like 'coloured sand' in the bottle. Each colour and therefore layer represents or symbolises something. It requires students to follow explicit instructions that you chunk (which leads in turn to order, as opposed to chaos!). The children also need to write what each colour represents and give careful thought to this.

The colours could symbolise a person, a character, a theme, a character trait, a place, a memory, a pet, a number, an element, emotions, an answer; whatever you like. It's excellent across the curriculum therefore and across key stages, but also for an SEMH activity. It can also aid memory and therefore revision.

Use old cardboard boxes to make stage sets of stories, or texts, or laboratories, or battles – anything relevant to what the students are learning. Some children with needs may find it easier to make what's in their mind's eye than write it, at least to begin with. Allow them be creative and use their imaginations.

Use empty little matchboxes covered in paper or silver foil, and give students paper to make a tiny scroll with a challenge (school-related, SEAL-based, short-term, long-term, whatever is appropriate), or a wish, hope or dream on it. Get them to pop it in the box and hold it first to their head & then to their heart, focusing on it. Tell them to take it home and squirrel it away somewhere, then look at it again in a month, a term, even a year, to remind them of their goal and whether they achieved it. Set aspirations. This can be linked to SEAL outcomes, academic outcomes, sport, mindfulness or even the Jewish concept of Tefillin. Be creative. I once taught a Year 10 boy who'd kept his in his blazer pocket (even transferred to a new blazer) since Year 7.

Sticky Notes

These can be stuck under chairs (mind the chewing gum), around the room, in books, on the board. You can write questions on some, corresponding answers on others.

They can have clues written on them, problems to solve, mysteries to investigate. You can write a character's name on one and, in pairs or other flexible groups, one child sticks the note to their forehead and then has to guess who they are by asking a variety of questions about the person, with the rest of the group answering those.

You can write map co-ordinates, or maths symbols, or historical figures, and get the kids to find their matching pair.

Sticky notes hold endless possibilities!

Props

Use these to create memorable learning experiences. Teach gothic fiction or spooky stories with plastic vampire teeth as you peer behind the classroom door. Pop a dribble of fake blood on your chin. Play moody music. Dress as famous scientists or a mathematician and get the kids to quiz you and look for clues as to who you are. Use masks, hats, costumes. Have the children dressing up – seniors and primary. Question them. Use and value the students' skills in flexible grouping, those who enjoy performing with those who have strong literacy, with another who does not, for example. This can be cross-curricular.

Pop Culture

Don't forget to tap into what the students are all about: their own generational culture. Use Netflix shows to teach maths or geography (property shows set in Los Angeles for example – the cost of those properties or the geography of them). Use reality TV (the misconceptions of some of its celebs regarding the true meaning of '100%', a phrase that is thrown around willy-nilly by whippersnappers). Dip into Tik Tok and use the current popular songs to teach. Remember when Kate Bush's 'Running Up That Hill' reached number 1 because of a Netflix show? Use those lyrics as poetry. Make relevant use of what's relevant to the students. This also shows you value their culture (even if you don't actually like it!). Use current gameshows, or old ones, or board game concepts.

Make Tik Toks. Have a YouTube channel. Tap into technology.

Image Enquiries

If done on PowerPoint these can do a slow reveal. Grab the students' attention. Or use an old game show format like Catchphrase to reveal sections of the image for correct answers.

Straws, Play Doh, Lego, Modelling Clay

You name it – use these resources from Year R to Year 11. Get students making earthquake-proof buildings, shaking the tables to test them. Have the children building hearts and organs, or modelling out of Play Doh and then labelling. Give explicit instructions to follow. Make Cornell notes afterwards. Put photos of the model in dual-coded knowledge organisers.

Use Lego in Geography – or English or RE, or any subject. Be creative about how you can. Don't be afraid to use resources we'd usually link to primary key stages for secondary students. Adaptive teaching sometimes needs some risks so we can see what works. If it doesn't, at least you've tried. If it does, brilliant!

Mystery Backpack

Fill a backpack with items, have the children guess who it belongs to. Where was it found? Why is there only one shoe in it? What's happened to the owner?

Have the students write their answers on pieces of paper, or mini-whiteboards and then go through them. Have them evaluating, justifying, comparing, inferring, applying skills and knowledge and so on.

Kim's Game

Have a tray with different relevant items on it. Show them to the students for a timed period, then cover it with a cloth and the students have to write down as many as they can remember. This is excellent for a variety of skills and outcomes, and also memory and embedding learning in a more playful – to begin with – way.

Lucky Dip Bag

This can be filled with anything and used for starters, or formative assessment, or creating flexible groups. It can contain questions and answers, or similes, or quizzes, SPaG, mysteries and so on.

If linked to pop culture, it can be a Bushtucker Trial bag – fill it with jelly and laminated 'would you rather' cards to pull out (e.g. would you rather be stranded with a survival box or an iPhone?), or formulas, or maths questions, or quotations, or lines of poetry.

Artefact Enquiries

Old science equipment, old postcards from charity shops, vintage glass bottles with glass stoppers, old books or old maps compared to today's maps. Stamps with different sovereigns on them, vintage ephemera, clothing from different eras, costume jewellery, religious artefacts, old photographs.

Things you have around your home. Who did they belong to? What do we know? What can we guess? How can we find out?

Music and Projectors

Use music, use your projector. Have a visual background of dance, or drama, or a roaring fire, or autumn leaves falling, or waves lapping a shoreline. Visit the world through Virtual Technology or Google Maps. Play different sounds – relaxing ones, classical music, experiment with the effect it may have on the class as well as on learning. Create moods, inspire the students, build atmosphere. Get them to have a go, too.

Optical Illusions

These can link to perspective, truth, fact, opinion, ethics, right and wrong, diversity, worldviews. Students love them but they also support learning – we can see things differently, but it doesn't mean we're wrong. And if we change our perspective a little, suddenly we can see something else, too.

Fortune Tellers

Younger children love these and older teens feel nostalgic for them.

Model one yourself first and give explicit instructions to the students. These can be used for revision or summarising a topic (and much else too - be creative). Use colour symbolically; emphasise the importance of precision folding the paper so that you can then open up different 'numbers' that are coded to reveal answers. Use it to scaffold, then remove the scaffold when ready.

For instructions, check out YouTube and have a search. There are loads of ideas.

Planting & Growing

Don't underestimate the joy that some children – just as much as adults – get from planting something and watching it grow.

This can be linked not only to science but to nurture. At its most basic, cress seeds in a classroom using damp cotton wool and empty cardboard egg cartons, provide real pleasure for youngsters and teenagers – the latter won't have done this for years and they'll love it. Link it to SEMH, to how we grow as people, to what we need to grow.

Make characters out of the egg cartons and have the cress grow as hair. Grow herbs to then cook with. Grow a tomato plant in your classroom. See if an avocado stone will take.

You can do it just for competitive spirit if necessary. Winner gets to (insert appropriate 'treat' here).

PART 3: PRACTICAL IDEAS FOR ADAPTING WITH PLAYFULNESS

Takeaways

- We are able to adapt not only our approaches using relational pedagogies, but also our **planning and resources**.
- **Playfulness** in learning can be lost as children get older because of testing and the pressures of the curriculum. However, ...
- ... Playfulness (as part of a **PACE** approach) can enable us to engage some students who find learning less accessible.
- Playfulness can therefore contribute to building our **inclusive classroom**.

COMING UP NEXT

- **Chapter 6** is going to look at how to **pull it all together** and use our learning from Chapters 1–5. We'll look at 2 plans for children with SEND, one from a primary key stage and one from secondary.
- By looking at the plans, we'll see how to use our knowledge of **SEND** (Chapters 1 and 2) by employing our **relational foundation** (Chapters 3 and 4) and **adapting** our teaching and our planning (Chapter 5). This will enable us to meet the needs in our classrooms, remove barriers to learning, and thereby ensure that our classrooms are **inclusive** places to learn.

Out of the Mouths of Staff

I've been teaching for about 15 years now and I've definitely got into the 'habit' of adaptive teaching. It's something that just makes sense. I think when I was younger I rushed through content too much maybe. I put myself under pressure to get through it all. I guess I've got more confident too and I'm able to stand back a bit, see the class and where they're at, recognise who needs what.

Class Teacher, Primary

Old-style differentiation is so different to what we do now and what I look for in a lesson. In some ways, it feels a bit embarrassing to look back at how it used to be. It was so prescriptive and unresponsive!

Head teacher, Primary

Adaptive teaching can be super simple but creative at the same time. It's totally about stopping to 'smell the roses' a bit and I like the challenge of unpicking 'how can I help X to get it?' What sequence of steps do I need to stop and repeat this in? It's deeply satisfying once the child understands and you know you've helped them. Those little sparkly lightbulbs going off – there's nothing better!

Head of Year, Seniors

For me, some strong adaptive teaching can be hard to evidence outside of the lesson as it is based entirely on the emerging need for adaptation as it happens in the lesson. For example – there could be a child who is usually very confident in their writing who is finding it a challenge to get started answering a particular question type, so you jot a sentence starter on a mini whiteboard for them and that is all the support that they need. It isn't always evident outside of that lesson (other than the child's growing confidence in completing that type of task/writing in the future), but the teaching responds immediately to the specific situation as it arises.

History Teacher, Seniors

Mini-whiteboards are something I use all the time. Whilst I know they have great Assessment for Learning potential and a lot of teachers use them to ask students to demonstrate understanding, or give an answer to something, in my classroom I find I use them more for me to write on than the students. It might be a key word that a student needs help with spelling – we can work it out on a mini-whiteboard together. Or, it could be some sentence starters, some bullet points of key ideas, a reminder of a structure for a paragraph or extended piece of writing. I find it useful to quickly write down things that I have verbally discussed with a student, so that they can refer back to it whilst completing work or discussing with a partner. Of course, I don't write down everything I discuss with every student on a mini-whiteboard, but I do find it useful for some key conversations, or to support specific students. Additionally, I use them to make 'now, next, then' notices for students, particularly those with identified SEND, who find it beneficial to have a visual cue of what is expected of them in the present moment and what is coming up next in the lesson. I also use mini whiteboards for 'beginning of lesson checklists' for a couple of students who find these useful to help them to settle into the start of the lesson, and for visual reminders of what is expected of a student at a given time – for example 'we are listening', 'we are discussing', 'we are writing'. The benefit of mini-whiteboards is that all of the above can either be done in advance – for example the beginning of lesson checklist, or sentence starters if the need is anticipated – or live in the lesson as the need for them arises.

Lead Teacher,
All-Through School

Notes

1 Available at: https://www.thesendcast.com/using-rosenshines-principles-of-instruction/
2 https://educationendowmentfoundation.org.uk/
3 https://www.britannica.com/topic/Blooms-taxonomy
4 https://www.researchgate.net/profile/Jim-Clark-10/publication/225249172_Dual
   _Coding_Theory_and_Education/links/542d58970cf277d58e8cc084/Dual-Coding
   -Theory-and-Education.pdf
5 Facebook: @*Theatre of Learning. Experiential RE.*

References

Blake, W. (1975 ed.). *The Marriage of Heaven and Hell*. Oxford: OUP.
Department for Education and Department of Health. (2019). *Early Career Framework*. Available at: https://assets.publishing.service.gov.uk/government/uploads/system/uploads/attachment_data/file/978358/Early-Career_Framework_April_2021.pdf

Education Endowment Foundation. (2020, updated 2021). *SEND in Mainstream Schools: A Guidance Report.* Available at: https://educationendowmentfoundation.org.uk/education-evidence/guidance-reports/send

Frayer, D., Frederick, W.C., and Klausmeier, H.J. (1969). *A Schema for Testing the Level of Cognitive Mastery.* Madison, WI: Wisconsin Center for Education Research.

Geertz, C. (1972). Deep Play. Notes on the Balinese Cockfight. *Daedalus,* 101(1), pp. 1-37.

Kolb, D.A. (1984). *Experiential Learning: Experience as the Source of Learning and Development.* Upper Saddle River, NJ: Prentice-Hall.

Pauk, W., Owens, R.J.Q. (2010). *How to Study in College* (10th ed.). Boston, MA: Wadsworth.

Phillips, S. (2013). *The Island. A Handbook for Teaching The Island in The Modern Classroom Using Enquiry Methods.* Available at: theatreoflearning@hotmail.co.uk

Rosenshine, B. (2012). Principles of Instruction: Research-Based Strategies That All Teachers Should Know. *American Educator,* 36(1), pp. 12-39. Available at: https://www.aft.org/sites/default/files/Rosenshine.pdf

Chapter Six

A Need-to-Know Basis

Pulling It All Together

As we commence the penultimate chapter of this book, let's look at how everything we have learnt so far, ties together.

We now know:

- That there are **4 Broad Areas of SEND** and that we can (and should) be **needs-led**, not just diagnosis-led.
- That 'teaching' today is **very different** to 'teaching' several years (and decades) ago - and we know a little of **why** this is.
- That **not all children** arrive in school ready to learn and ready to trust us, and that **relational pedagogies** support this.
- That relational pedagogies are **intrinsic** to inclusive classrooms and inclusive schools.
- That we must therefore use our relational pedagogies to adapt our **approaches** to children.
- And that we must then adapt our **teaching** and our **planning** to meet the needs in our classrooms, thereby making them fully **inclusive**.

In order then to embed this, we are going to look at **2 plans for children with SEND**, such as those that you might be given in school, so that we can see exactly where we'd use our own learning from this book to ensure that their needs are met in our inclusive classroom.

In this chapter, we'll consider:

Chapter 6	Summary
Documents of Support - How Would You *Now* Use Them?	This will include an exemplar of 2 **documents detailing needs** that our Learning Support Departments might give us, in this case a '**Pupil Passport**' (known by various names). We need to remember our model of **Cause and Effect**, with a recap of the **Toolkit** for building our inclusive classroom. Given everything that we have covered in our previous chapters, how would you use the documents? How can you recognise what to use and where?
How Will I Juggle All This?!	Why it's easier than we think to teach in an adaptive and responsive manner - particularly as opposed to traditional 'differentiation'. **We can do this!**

DOI: 10.4324/b23417-7

Documents of Support - How Will You Now Use Them?

So, you have your relational foundation, you know what adaptive teaching is, and you have some practical ideas of how to do it. However, when it comes to it and we are at the chalk-face as opposed to on the book's page, **it is daunting**.

It isn't really *until* we're doing it, that we realise *we can do it*. Just as we somehow end up knowing literally hundreds of names by the end of Autumn One, we also quickly realise who needs some extra support. Often, you'll already be in receipt of that knowledge via your SENDCO. Hopefully they are very present in school (though possibly rather overwhelmed and generally a bit stressed. Throw chocolate at them).

How important do you think learning names is to children **feeling included**?

How do you ensure correct **pronunciation**?

How important do you think knowing a name is to **supporting** learning?

It's been a common idea throughout history and within ancient beliefs that knowing someone's name gives you **authority**. We need to be authoritative in school. When a young person is standing on their chair, or sprinting down a corridor in the opposite direction to you, knowing their name can certainly help! **How** else is it helpful, aside from being able to report the mischief? Have you ever worked in a school where the children called staff by their first names? What was this like?

Do staff in your school refer to one another as 'Sir' or 'Miss', or 'Mr X' and 'Ms X', even when the children aren't around? Is this down to practicality in a large school, or habit, or laziness? Does it make a difference?

These days, the kinds of systems that we have access to in school make it very easy to look at our students and see who has already been identified as needing extra support. You may use a system that has a **photographic seating plan** for example, and at the click of a button a symbol pops up telling you which of those young people has SEND. At the click then of another button, or the hover of a cursor, you may be taken directly to the **documents** that will explain what those SEND are, what the **strengths** of the child are, and what **strategies** you should utilise to support needs and adapt your teaching accordingly.

These documents will be the condensed version of whatever format they started out as. Your SENDCO may have received an Educational Psychology (EP) report for example, and then taken the suggested strategies from this and put them into a '**Pupil Passport**', or other similar but differently named document that makes it easy for you to see what's what. They may have observed the child in classes, spoken to other staff, parents, external agencies and so forth, and then disseminated information. The child may have a diagnosed need (see Chapter 2 for a reminder of the **4 Broad Areas**

of Need) and they may even have a legally binding document of support, such as the EHCPs (or similar but differently-named documents, depending on where one teaches) that we also looked at in Chapter 2.

All these reports and documents will be combined and condensed to make up whatever you'll have in front of you as a class teacher, and these are your **starting point**. However, in the midst of this, do not forget to alert your SENDCO via whatever system they have in place, to any possible unidentified needs in your classroom. It may be that there are none and a child just finds something challenging, or too easy, or they're a bit of a day-dreamer, but raise it just to be sure. Early intervention, preventative approaches, and being **needs-led**, as discussed in Chapter 2, are all crucial. If you are unsure of anything, ask your SENDCO or someone else in the Learning Support Department. It may also be that a child in your class has a 1:1, in which case that adult will be a fantastic source of knowledge about the student, and someone with whom you should work very closely to best support them. (There will be more on this in Chapter 7.)

It is also worth bearing in mind that **pupil voice** is a central tenet of all successful Pupil Passports – just as it is a central tenet of inclusion. Your SENDCO or Learning Support staff will be the people who can advise you on this and who often write passports, but equally you may need to contribute to one yourself (particularly in primary classes). Involving the child whilst you write it can lead to wonderful conversations about their own perspectives, needs, and feelings, and this in itself is not only inclusive but key to building our relationships.

A WORD ON EDUCATION, HEALTH, AND CARE PLANS (EHCPS)

(Or legally binding documents of support/plans, by any other name)

For information regarding any form of **legally binding** document of support, we can look back to **Chapter 2** and see examples there. These documents will be large and very detailed, but that is not for you to worry about if you are a busy class teacher in a mainstream school. You are highly unlikely to use an EHCP in its entirety.

Instead, your SENDCO will condense the strategies and outcomes from the document for you to use in order to support any child with an EHCP in your classroom, for example, in a Pupil Passport. Do not be daunted by this; seek support from specialist staff in school and always ensure that you **get to know** the child really well. Include parents in conversations and of course any 1:1 staff (relationships with both will be considered further in Chapter 7) and do make sure that the child feels included in their learning experiences. This **feeling of inclusion**, of actively feeling included in the classroom, is the absolute crux of what we are aiming for.

Using a Pupil Passport

(AKA 'PEN Portraits', 'Pupil Profile', or any document of support outside of a legally binding plan)

Using our learning from Chapters 1-5, let's now look at two examples of Pupil Passports and what they may contain. You'll either be given these or expected to find electronic copies on your school system. Printing them and highlighting them/annotating them may be helpful. As we look at them, ask yourself what you would do to support the child?

Exemplar 1

Our first example is for a **Year 2 child**. This student has **needs around SEMH** with a complex background of childhood **trauma and neglect**.

Subsequently, our **relational and trauma-informed approaches** and our **unconditional positive regard (UPR)** really come to the fore here. Teachers would not be bound by what is in this document – we should always try to be creative and adaptive to what we see, and we can then update the Pupil Passport with what does or does not work well.

Take a look and consider: **how would you adapt your teaching to support Reva?**

Student Details	My Strengths	What Do You Need to Know About Me?	Strategies to Help Me	Using relational pedagogy, the advice of the EEF and Rosenhine, and Playfulness, how would you adapt your teaching to support Reva? *Some have been filled in for you – what else could you do?*
Name: Reva Year: 2 Class: Robins Area of Need: SEMH (incl trauma recovery). Reva is a Looked After Child and lives with her nan.	I like listening to and telling **jokes.** I know lots of facts about **sea creatures.** I am great at **drawing** using different pens and pencils. I am in a **football** team! Once I am **calm** I am able to listen really well and follow instructions. I will **always encourage and congratulate** children when they succeed.	I sometimes refuse to talk to adults as a **coping mechanism.** I need **time to think and reflect** before speaking with an adult about my emotions and actions. I struggle to **regulate my emotions.** I can become frustrated and this can lead to my hurting others. I understand this is not the right choice but **struggle to control** this in the moment. All **behaviour is communication**, if I am doing something I shouldn't it is because I am trying to tell you something about how I am feeling. This does **not excuse** my behaviour, but it **does give a reason for it.**	I believe the work I produce is **not good enough** and will therefore scribble over my book out of frustration and being upset; this is a fear of failure as opposed to 'bad behaviour'. I respond better with an adult support by my side offering **positive praise. High challenge with high support.** A **PACE approach** that emphasises **play.** Learning through play as much as possible – Reva should have the same or similar LOs to the class, but you can **adapt** her method of achieving them. Give Reva as **many ways to record answers** as possible.	Reva can use the **self-regulation station** that has been set up by adults in class. It has a soft cushion, mindful activities, a squishy and an egg timer. Reva can record answers verbally on an iPad, using chalk on a board, using a mini-whiteboard, or on a piece of paper, with **increasing encouragement** to write them. Reva shares footballing success with the class and brings in photos! If a child is sad in class, Reva can be asked to cheer them up with a joke. **NVC** and **restorative meetings** are used with Reva and other children once the situation and emotions have **settled.**

Student Details	My Strengths	What Do You Need to Know About Me?	Strategies to Help Me	Using relational pedagogy, the advice of the EEF and Rosenhine, and Playfulness, how would you adapt your teaching to support Reva? *Some have been filled in for you – what else could you do?*
			Self-regulation station – Reva needs time and space to self-regulate rather than running out of classroom. Reva can **choose** each day if she wants to attend lunch club or the hall for lunch – with the understanding that she stays in the same place for the whole session. Bringing a **transition object** in from home to help her feel close to her family. Adult support to complete tasks throughout the day. Boost Reva's **self-confidence.** Interventions put in place by SENDCO to support Reva (ELSA, Time to Talk, 1:1 reading, writing).	Adults must use a calm, **relational approach** when dealing with Reva's actions. Follow **NVC strategies** when speaking with her. She needs to spend time with adults **AFTER** the event when she is calm, to discuss what has happened so she feels she is listened to and then have time to learn from her mistakes e.g. apologising. Give Reva **time to settle** after an incident (at least ten minutes). Her emotions are too heightened to deal with her behaviour in the moment. Flexible grouping – Reva is a keen artist and congratulates others when they succeed. Chances for Reva to succeed are regularly built into her learning. Tasks to be set out on Reva's **mini-whiteboard.**

Takeaways from Reva's Pupil Passport

When we first read the passport, it can seem daunting, but actually it's just a matter of being **responsive**.

1) Reva needs a relational approach with **PACE** and playfulness. **Accept** that Reva has suffered traumatic events in her infancy. Be **curious** about her, use **empathy**. Remember the scientific effects of neglect and trauma on children's **brain development** (Chapters 3 and 4).
2) **NVC and 'Name It to Tame It'** (see Chapter 4) will support us in communicating with Reva.
3) Because of childhood trauma, giving Reva **clear**, **safe** choices to make, so she feels some control, can be supportive. She needs high challenge and high support (see Chapter 4).
4) Reva needs a 'regulation station' – this can be as simple as a **small safe space** with a cushion and squishy toy.
5) Reva needs a 'task board' – this can be as simple as a **mini-whiteboard** on which you write 'now' and 'next' tasks.
6) Reva's self-confidence needs boosting – **worthy praise** and pointing out the **positives**, celebrating with her, telling Reva's nan the positives at the end of the day; remember our **relational foundational**.
7) If Reva has done something she shouldn't, then this is not ignored but we **wait** for her to calm down and for the situation to deescalate before we then come back to it. Reva will then be better able to listen and learn.

8) Behaviour is communication – how can our **Cause and Effect** model help us here to best support Reva?

Exemplar 2

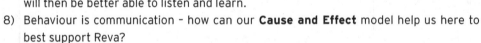

Our second exemplar of a Pupil Passport is for a **Year 9** boy who has **no diagnosed needs** but whose behaviour (the effect) has recently meant that his parents and teachers have become concerned as to whether there is an unidentified need (or cause).

A SEND teacher has subsequently met with the student and his parents, observed him in class, discussed his progress and current presentation with subject teachers and the Head of Year, and then devised the following strategies for supporting him.

If we consider the **9 areas of neuro-development** that we looked at in Chapter 2, then we can see that this SEND teacher believes the student may have needs around **Energy Levels**, **Attention and Impulse Control**, and **Adaptability and Flexibility**. Following a needs-led approach, the support detailed in the Pupil Passport can therefore be put in place and reviewed regularly to see if the lad's engagement and behaviour improve. This follows the SEND Code of Practice's 'assess-plan-do-review' model.

Take a look and consider: **how would you adapt your teaching to support Cayden?**

Student Details	My Strengths	What Do You Need to Know About Me?	Strategies to Help Me	Using relational pedagogy, the advice of the EEF and Rosenhine, and Playfulness, how would you adapt your teaching to support Cayden? *Some have been filled in for you – what else could you do?*
Name: Cayden Year: 9 Class: 9B Area of Need: energy levels, attention and impulse control, and adaptability and flexibility.	I am a lovely young gentleman with a lot to offer, and I am a keen musician. I am a keen gymgoer! I can be very productive when my attention is captured. I play 5 instruments – bass, guitar, violin, piano, and drums. I have an excellent sense of humour and a strong friendship group.	I fidget which I find helps me to focus – it **doesn't always mean I am not listening.** Often, this will take the form of tapping my fingers on tables. I have had a neuro-developmental profile completed by Mr X in co-production with my parents. The areas in which I have some additional need for support are: **energy levels, attention and impulse control, and adaptability and flexibility.** I find it **hard to attend to activities** in lessons and challenging to concentrate.	Use **mindful flexible grouping.** Consider a careful seating plan. Cayden would be better placed nearer to the teacher so that they **can interact regularly** with him and check in regularly. Teachers should discuss this Pupil Passport **with** Cayden and devise a **discreet signal** in collaboration with him that will enable him to regain focus if he becomes distracted. Keep work **mindfully paced** for Cayden – not in a manner that means going too fast, but keep work to short bursts. Do not give Cayden a title and just set him off to work.	Cayden should be **carefully seated** in class, away from distractions. He's a keen scribe which works well in groups where he also encourages others with their handwriting. A **discreet signal** is used: a tap on the desk. This was decided with Cayden so that he had some ownership of this. If a piece of extended writing is required, we do not stop with Cayden's first answer or draft; we **layer** more content in, after feedback and reflection. Where extended writing is necessary, it is in bursts. This **chunking** works well. **Scaffolding** is achieved through sticky notes and mini-whiteboard notes from myself. I often give Cayden the title and then ask him to briefly jot down ideas for the introduction. I then return and we review.

Student Details	My Strengths	What Do You Need to Know About Me?	Strategies to Help Me	Using relational pedagogy, the advice of the EEF and Rosenhine, and Playfulness, how would you adapt your teaching to support Cayden? *Some have been filled in for you – what else could you do?*
		I respond better in subjects that are **practical** – art, music, PE, and so on – and therefore, if other lesson resources are adapted to involve some practical element, I will find it easier to access and attend to.	**Layer** written work. Scaffold written work – for an evaluative argument for example, e.g.: If America banned guns, then it would be a safer place. Do you agree or disagree? – **Know when to remove the scaffold!**	**Explicit** and **repeated** instruction – with Cayden repeating back to me – is used.
		I do not always sleep well – my mind is always on the go.	Provide Cayden with **discreet movement breaks** – so not called 'movement breaks' in front of others.	I set a time limit and give him **timely reminders** whilst he's working. I then move Cayden onto the next part of the work. This may be entirely different to how other students are working but it supports Cayden and leads to better outcomes in terms of his learning and his presenting behaviour in class.
		If work looks too long, I will be inclined to avoid it – tasks must be broken down (see strategies).	Make a **conscious effort** to start sentences and instructions with Cayden's name.	I incorporate **discreet movement breaks** for Cayden, taking the form of 'can you go and grab me the textbook please' ... 'can you just write that idea on the board' ... and so on.
		If you have a good relationship with me, I will respond well to you.	Allow Cayden to **discreetly doodle** on a piece of scrap paper or in the back of his book – it helps him focus and he says he does this in lessons anyway and teachers often don't notice. Don't assume he's not listening therefore if you see him doing this!	I also incorporate more **active learning** in class – for example, Vote With Your Feet ('go to the left of the room if you think ... go to the right if you think ... stay in the middle if you think ...' etc).
		Use a **PACE** approach – this is a long-term investment.		

Takeaways from Cayden's Pupil Passport

Cayden's passport has lots of information on it but we **don't need** to process all of this at once. We can print it and save a copy in our planner and highlight bits and bobs to try, plus we don't need to implement all of it because it's not prescriptive.

Instead, because we are teaching **adaptively**, we can see that Cayden has needs around his attention and his ability to attend to tasks, and so it's common sense that we can't give Cayden a massive essay title and expect him to just run with it. As with Reva, it is a matter of being **responsive**:

1) Use a **relational approach** with **PACE**.
2) Include Cayden in discussion about what will support him - be **curious**.
3) **Break tasks down.** This needn't be onerous; use sticky notes, jot it down in Cayden's book, write it on a mini-whiteboard, and so on.
4) Use **layering** - build a piece of work up from its initial draft. Keep returning to it.
5) If using scaffolding, once Cayden understands, **remove** it.
6) **Check in** with Cayden, get him to **repeat** instructions and check his **understanding**. Use cognitive and metacognitive activities (see Chapter 5).
7) Sit Cayden where you can see him and keep an eye on him. Say his name at the start of a sentence if it's directed towards him. Use **flexible grouping** that's mindful of who he's sitting with and what outcome you want.
8) **Refocus** Cayden whenever necessary, **accept** that he needs to fidget or move about sometimes, and that it's hard for him to attend to tasks for extended periods independently.

With both Reva and Cayden, what we need to do is **respond** to whatever they present with. **Adapt** your lesson accordingly for them. We can see in both the guidance of both **Rosenshine Principles** and the **EEF's SEND report** (see Chapter 5). We can also see our **relational pedagogies** throughout (see Chapter 4).

If Cayden, for example, looks like he's daydreaming or he's about to blow the insert of his biro out of said biro and into the direction of his mate's back, respond to that with refocusing techniques, gaining his attention, using your agreed signal, going to stand near his chair whilst you're engaged in whole-class delivery, and so forth.

If Reva does not understand a question, reframe it. If she gets frustrated, remind her to use her regulation station, and speak with her, using NVC, once she's calm.

In essence, we bend to the needs we are presented with.

When you were first training and you watched experienced members of staff teach, did you think it might actually be quite **easy** (because the teacher made it look that way!)?

How long did it take you when you first taught a class to begin **feeling** the vibrations underneath it and to start managing those like a seasoned conductor? How long does it take you to now, each September, when you gain a new class/es?

That 'conducting' is what **adaptive teaching** is all about. Some of it is **preventative** - if we know the students - much can be **reactive**, in the moment, because that's the nature of learning. It's all about our **flexibility**.

How Will I Juggle All This?!

A jolly good question.

It seems particularly insurmountable when we consider that the average number of children with SEND (that have been identified) teeters at around 16%.[1] However, adaptive teaching is not about increasing workload - and, having that relational foundation to your classroom automatically puts you at an advantage; one where you know your students, you recognise and empathise with their needs, and they will recognise this in you.

We can sometimes open our online system in school, see a Pupil Passport such as Cayden's, and wish to run a mile in the opposite direction and go and find a job that does not feel as though it is, on the difficulty scale, up there with herding kittens around an open field all day. But would that job give us the same satisfaction as when Cayden and Reva begin to respond to us, to engage, to learn? *No!* And just because the Pupil Passport looks daunting and nigh on impossible to achieve, it really isn't once you just get into the **habit of adaptive teaching**.

The Habit of Adaptive Teaching

Much of what is in the Pupil Passport will become *second nature* to you, it will become habitual and you'll create a veritable smorgasbord of techniques that you can pull out of your inclusive classroom toolkit as and when you recognise the need to. Adaptive teaching is responsive teaching.

It is about being **mindful** and remembering to use our **common sense** which, on the spur of a busy moment, can sometimes feel really challenging. So, we must practise these methods of support and, by doing so, they'll become part of the ebb and flow of our classroom.

Cayden, for example, isn't always going to need a writing frame. Remember, we are *adapting*. Once he's mastered his persuasive writing or whatever it is he's learning, you can remove the scaffold. This is part of our inclusive classroom that comes and goes as needed. It's not permanent. (If, however, you were to remove your relational approach and your UPR from Reva at any time, then that would be nothing short of disastrous).

If we continue to consider the writing frame then, let us also then bear in mind the **ECF information** that we referred to in Chapter 1, and remember that adaptive teaching is **not** about creating different resources for all children in the classroom. Cayden may need a writing frame for an evaluative argument, but that needn't mean you having to type it up and print out something different for him. You may well wish to keep a bank of writing frames somewhere in your room that you can whip out at a moment's notice, but you can also:

1.) Use a pack of **sticky notes**, write 'what is the argument about?' on one and stick it on Cayden's page. Tell him to jot down ideas, say you'll be back in 3 minutes to check in, move on to another child.

2.) Return to Cayden when you said you would (be **consistent**), check what he's been up to, live mark/feedback where needed, and then write '2 opinions of your own', stick it on his page, repeat the pattern. Others in the class may excel at simply following whatever instruction you've written on the board, or what's on the Power Point, but Cayden needs that structure, that focus, those reminders.

3.) Alternatively, write one on a **mini-whiteboard**, wipe it off and replace it when you return. Once Cayden knows the drill, you can just write 'what?' on the first sticky note or the mini-whiteboard, eventually removing the scaffolding altogether because Cayden can now attend to the piece of work at hand, knowing how to break it down, and just having check-ins from you as you work the room.

This is a key skill in teaching; **to adapt to what we see in front of us**. And really knowing the students is a vast part of it.

As a SEND specialist, it is incredibly disheartening to go into a classroom and see no adaptations whatsoever. I've seen children with EHCPs sat at the back of classrooms, alone with a Learning Support Assistant (LSA) who has found getting any collaboration out of the class teacher akin to removing an especially stubborn verruca.

We must employ our **UPR** and our **consistent relational approaches** to adapt to and accommodate the needs in our classroom. We absolutely *must* empathise and recall what it is like when we can't access something ourselves. How would we expect to be treated? To do any less than this is just a blatant disregard for the children and young people in front of us. Much as we are important (our own oxygen masks first and so forth, à la Chapter 1), it is nevertheless the **children who come first**.

HOW NOT TO DO IT

I once visited a school where I saw a teacher tell his Year 9 class (that had a high number of children with needs present), that 'YES IT'S HARD BUT LIFE IS HARD!' The same teacher then stood over a table of youngsters and requested that one girl give him the answer to the sum on the board. The girl just blinked in stunned response, only to be greeted by a huge sigh - no support, no chivvying along, no encouragement. This kind of non-relational, judgmental, humiliating classroom practice is hopefully rare, but it should serve to remind us why our empathy - PACE - is so important.

If we imagine being adults and experiencing a member of SLT speaking to us like that in front of all the staff during a whole-school meeting, then we'd doubtless feel both humiliated and fuming. It would not be motivational, other than spurring us to fantasise about the kind of email we'd send them should we win the lottery (hopefully after having had our numbers officially confirmed). The experience would burn; it's a **memorable learning experience** but precisely the wrong kind.

CHAPTER 6

A Need-to-Know Basis: Pulling It All Together

Takeaways

- Our **SENDCO** is our main port of call and plans for support will usually be stored digitally on our school systems.
- We can use the plans for support, incorporating **our knowledge** of relational pedagogies, adaptive teaching (the EEF and Rosenshine), and adapting our planning using Playfulness.
- **Adaptive** teaching becomes **habitual** – we will recognise when extra support is needed and we can try a whole variety of different strategies because we now **know a whole variety of different strategies**!

COMING UP NEXT

In **Chapter 7**, our final chapter, we'll look at inclusion for all stakeholders – including parents and carers, and the other adults in your classroom.

Out of the Mouths of Staff

As a SENDCO, it's brilliant when staff are passionate about supporting children with SEND. I love it when they show an interest, they want to unpick needs, and they try different strategies. However, I do get annoyed with the minority of staff who take no notice of the students' plans or needs. I understand that staff are busy but this is their job – and adaptive teaching is about adapting to all needs, not only those that come under the SEND umbrella. It's easy to make small but impactful changes.

SENDCO, Secondary School

I think working within SEND is all about winning hearts and minds, and building relationships – be it with children, families or staff. Once you've done that, you can go on to build anything, because you're building it together.

SEND Teacher, Primary

As a class teacher, I find our school's digital systems really helpful. It's very different to when I first taught. I remember the SENDCO then would send out a paper list each year of your class, with needs detailed in a column next to the child's name. To be honest, I wouldn't then hear much else from the SENDCO for the year, let alone have a bank of strategies to try. Maybe that was just my experience and other schools were different, but since the Code of Practice in 2015, things have changed – for the better!

Class Teacher, Primary

The most helpful thing for me by far, is to involve the child directly, be in contact with their parent or carer too, and find out what's working and what isn't.

Maths Teacher, Secondary

I work in a special school so it's much smaller and we know the children really well. We are nothing if not flexible and responsive! You couldn't do the job if you weren't! I'd say that getting to know the children is the number one most meaningful thing you can do.

Teacher, Special School

Note

1 Available at: https://assets.publishing.service.gov.uk/government/uploads/system/uploads/attachment_data/file/1082518/Special_educational_needs_publication_June_2022.pdf

Chapter Seven

What About the Adults?

Parents, Carers, and Support Staff

And so, suddenly we find ourselves commencing the final chapter of this book. It doesn't seem so long ago that we were just starting out, yet suddenly here we are. We now have knowledge about SEND, relational pedagogies, and adaptive teaching techniques tucked firmly under our educational belts, as well as, hopefully, an honest-to-goodness under-standing and passion about why we need to use them.

In this final chapter, we are going to take a look at stakeholders other than the children and young people - because true inclusion should include us all. There are a whole host of people we could talk about, from governors to site staff, but for our purposes here we are going to focus firstly on our support staff and, secondly, on parents and carers. The latter have been mentioned throughout this book and we are going to complete it by considering them - and the relationships that we need to build and nurture with them.

So, coming up:

Chapter 7	Summary
Support Staff and How to Work Effectively with Them	Here, we'll consider the guidance of the EEF once again regarding their 5th recommendation of 'working effectively with teaching assistants', and we'll also think about how your relational pedagogies come into play here. Throughout this book we have ended each chapter with some words from staff, but a significant portion of this chapter will be taken directly from interviews with teaching assistants, in their own words.
Parents and Carers	It goes without saying that parents and carers are entrusting us with their children - we can and must never underestimate this. Again, our relational pedagogies and our emotional intelligence should be at the fore here.

Support Staff and How to Work Effectively with Them

Teaching Assistants (TAs), Learning Support Assistants (LSAs), 1:1s, or support staff in our classrooms by any other name would smell as sweet. I've not quite nailed it like Shakespeare, but you get the drift - there are myriad names out there these days for support staff but, whatever they're called, they're generally a massive boon to the room. Often, although not always, TA is a primary term and LSA may be more common in secondary settings. Either way, it's great to have their support.

DOI: 10.4324/b23417-8

Children with an Education, Health, and Care Plan often have a TA or LSA which is funded by their EHCP. Some primary classes are fortunate enough to have a permanent TA, others share across year groups, and in secondary classes, there will usually be zilch in the way of support unless a child with an EHCP is in the lesson, accompanied by their LSA. It is worth noting that the language of referring to support staff as '1:1s' is being moved away from by some schools and local authorities. This is for various reasons, not least that it can give the impression that a supportive adult should be 'glued' to one child, whereas this can be detrimental, leading to a lack of independence. It also means that the key adult feels unable to support other children in the class.

Support staff such as LSAs and TAs get to know the children really well, which is incredibly helpful for you as a teacher. They may deliver small group interventions, or 1:1 interventions, they will have a more intricate knowledge of a child's disability or medical need, and they will also be a source of support for parents. In short, our support staff are crucial in helping us to remove barriers to children's learning, and they will often also have an amazing relationship with the young people in our classrooms.

How many support staff do you have in your classroom? This will depend on whether you are a primary or secondary specialist, and how many children with an EHCP may be in your class at any given time.

Have you ever received **training** at school regarding how to make the most effective use of the support staff in your classroom?

If you're in a secondary setting, do you know the names and **specialisms** of each member of support staff who may be in your classroom during the week? Do you utilise those skills in a particular manner? (e.g. knowing that an LSA is especially strong in numeracy, or another is an excellent artist.)

Making the Best Use of Support Staff in Your Classroom

It should go without saying by now that the absolute best thing you can do, is to start building a relationship with TAs, or with any support staff coming into your inclusive classroom, because it's all about being and feeling included.

Some support staff will be more confident and experienced than others. For example, if you're a secondary school teacher, then you may only see an LSA once or twice a week, and they might not feel confident enough to come and introduce themselves to you. We forget sometimes as teachers that we are perceived (believe it or not) as being in a position of some authority. We can therefore seem intimidating to other stakeholders - including parents and support staff - so should endeavour to welcome TAs into our rooms, introduce ourselves, find out and remember their names, and ensure they are a part of the learning processes in our classrooms.

Once this is established, we can move forwards more successfully with the real reason the support staff are with us: enabling the children to succeed. **The Education Endowment Foundation (EEF)**, whose work around SEND in mainstream schools was referred to in Chapter 5, is also extremely helpful to us here.

The EEF's Report: 'Making Best Use of Teaching Assistants' (2018)

I returned to university not so long ago, part-time, to complete my NASENCO[1] qualification. Given that this is post-grad, and that you must have Qualified Teacher Status, the average age of those enrolled is somewhat older than those embarking on, for example, their first graduate rodeo. The hilarity of our wonderful course leader gamely showing us the Student Union Bar, as we shuffled around our campus tour like dinosaurs being paraded in the bemused faces of 18-year-olds who can still stand up without groaning audibly, has yet to leave me.

The course is weighty to say the least, and the assignments culminate in a research project. Plenty of people who successfully gained NASENCO pre-2018 completed said projects around how to best deploy TAs but, since then, the EEF's report around **Making the Best Use of Teaching Assistants** has led to it being an ill-advised choice, such is the comprehensive nature of said report. Basically, the heavy lifting has been done, it's all there for schools to implement, and NASENCO enrolees the country over have had to scratch that choice off their list, and focus their research efforts elsewhere.

Happily for us, it means that – as with the EEF's SEND report – we have clear guidance, which can be found in short on page 3 of the report, and is summarised below. There are **7 recommendations**. If you fancy getting a slightly more detailed picture but don't wish to read the whole report (your SENDCO will have read it, and this is not something you need to do), then I fully recommend downloading the EEF's Recommendations Poster.[2] Although hopefully, your SENDCO has kindly provided you with a copy.

Making the Best Use of Teaching Assistants
(The Education Endowment Foundation, 2018, pages 10-11)
You will see where the EEF's Guidance Report for SEND in Mainstream Schools (2020) (Chapter 5) links in here

The effective use of TAs under everyday classroom conditions				The effective use of TAs in delivering structured interventions out of class		Integrating learning from work led by teachers and TAs
1. TAs should not be used as an informal teaching resource for low attaining pupils.	2. Use TAs to add value to what teachers do, not replace them.	3. Use TAs to help pupils develop independent learning skills and manage their own learning.	4. Ensure TAs are fully prepared for their role in the classroom.	5. Use TAs to deliver high-quality one-to-one and small-group support using structured interventions.	6. Adopt evidence-based interventions to support TAs in their small group and one-to-one instruction.	7. Ensure explicit connections are made between learning from everyday classroom teaching and structured interventions.

What does this mean for us then?
As class teachers, we need to:

Remember that nothing beats High-Quality Teaching for removing barriers to learning (Chapter 5). Ensure that TAs and the children they support are being and feeling included. Remember, it's all about inclusion.	Never speak to the child 'through' the TA – don't lose sight of the child. Collaborate with the TA – they are not a replacement for us working with children with SEND in the class.	Support our TAs in helping students to become as independent in learning as they can. Encourage TAs to use (and model for them) cognitive and metacognitive talk (Chapter 5) with children.	The SENDCO has a responsibility here re training and making time for TAs to meet with staff, but you can also support – collaborate fully with the TA. Share outcomes, resources, planning, and key concepts.	Again, the SENDCO will have impact here, but if you're able to then support the TA in delivering very structured, rigorously planned, high-quality interventions can have meaningful impact on closing identified gaps – as opposed to the more wishy-washy variety of "let's do a bit of spelling and grammar' interventions.	Basically, if your school isn't using one of the few evidence-based programmes for intervention, then whatever is being used should replicate those. Your SENDCO and Learning Support Department should be co-ordinating this, but it's still worth your knowing. Ask the TA what they're following, engage with them, listen, support wherever possible, collaborate. This links to the 7th recommendation.	Find time to liaise with whichever TA is delivering interventions to your student/s, whether in primary or in a secondary subject area. This is a key part of inclusion. Interventions aren't separate from what goes on in class. They should explicitly link to, supplement, build upon, embed, and expand the learning taking place in the classroom.

Which of the EEF's 7 recommendations do you **already** do well?

Can you recognise areas in which you could do more? **How** will you go about doing so?

Is your **SENDCO** ensuring that these 7 recommendations – or similar – happen in school already?

As can be seen then, our support staff are a vital part of the inclusion process – and we need to ensure that we are being as inclusive of them as we are of the children and young people in our classrooms. However, we also need to ensure that neither the children – nor ourselves – become overly dependent on them.

In the spirit of inclusion, the following are a host of soundbites from a variety of TAs, some working in secondary settings, some in primary settings. The support staff were asked what they found most helpful from teachers, how they were made to feel included and valued in classrooms, and how they'd used relational approaches with their students.

Out of the Mouths of Support Staff

I find it most helpful when teachers liaise with me prior to the lesson about what we'll be doing. I work in a senior school and so I see a lot of staff – several are excellent asking my opinion about resources and how to make them accessible for my student who has an EHCP. I try hard to ensure I 'step back' once he is feeling more confident and he's working independently.

When I first meet a teacher, I do make a point of seeking them out and letting them know my student's needs, his likes and dislikes, any possible triggers and so forth.

I work in a primary school and I remember being sat at a table with my student who had an EHCP and also 2 other students who had learning differences but not EHCPs. It felt like we'd been segregated from the rest of the class. Eventually the SENDCO had a word with the class teacher and we then had some training around 'flexible grouping'. I hadn't been confident enough on my own to say that it felt like the teacher spoke to me and then ignored our little table for long periods of time. As a TA, you assume the teachers know best and they might think you're rude for making any suggestions.

I once worked with a deaf child who had delayed fine motor skills. His passion was drama, and he would only participate fully if I got involved with him. Therefore, I ended up taking a drama GCSE alongside him at the age of 47! We went to open our certificates together, and to see his face when he opened his envelope on Results' Day to discover he'd passed, was just priceless for me. Happily, I'd passed it too, and he was equally as thrilled for me! It's a special memory.

I find it really helpful in my primary school when I'm able to meet with my class teacher during their PPA time and we go through the planning and the intended learning outcomes together. I'm really lucky that our SENDCO has organised this and that I feel valued by the SLT and the class teachers. It really helps me to understand what we're aiming for, to get a bigger picture of the learning, and to then support the students to the best of my ability. I love my job and I feel fully included in every part of school life!

I work in a secondary school with both a student who has an EHCP and some who do not. I find it really helpful when teachers print off any Power Points in advance – it means my student has it there in front of him and we can flick back and forth.

I've definitely noticed that some teachers adapt their teaching more than others – I get a good overview from being around the school due to working in Key Stage 4.

It's important to use distraction techniques with some teens, I find. It's all part of building a relationship. Some can be resistant to working with an adult – they don't want to 'stand out' – so I'll occasionally engage them instead about something like their hair ('I love your curls, how did you do those?') and then slide in a bit of learning support. I'll also remember little things about them, like how they were planning their weekend, then I'll ask them about it the next week. Building those relationships then means they're more trusting of me, more comfortable with me, and more open to being supported.

I'm in a primary class and sometimes I'll support by stealth! There are some children who are just really resistant to my helping them but, because I'm not attached to anyone in the class, I have discovered that, for example, explicitly pointing out what a child has done well – when they are sat next to a child who's resistant to me but struggling – actually works really well in supporting the one who is struggling. They always listen in and then they take it on board and will often edit their work or rethink things. I've been a TA for a long time, and I suppose you start adapting what you're doing just like class teachers do.

Parents and Carers

Throughout this book, we've considered families, parents, and carers. We've also looked at the importance of avoiding blame, or inducing shame. When it comes to families and parents, we can speak with fact - as our RP shows us, we need to be explicit - but we must never speak with judgement. There is a clear difference between the two.

How often do you make **positive** calls home?

How often do you make contact with home due to poor behaviour?

Have you ever used a **preventative approach** to making contact home – realising swiftly that at some point you may well need to make contact that's going to sound negative, and therefore ensuring that you've made some positive contact early on? This can make a huge difference in terms of the success of your eventual working relationship with a parent or carer.

Building Bridges and Breaking Barriers

Out of the people that I spoke to whilst writing this book, including parents, teachers, Educational Psychologists, and lecturers in SEND and inclusion, the most consistent factor mentioned was that relationships between teachers and parents were crucial in getting the best outcomes for children and young people – and that the sooner those relationships were built, the better.

This is no surprise to us with our knowledge of relational approaches and the Harvard study into Adult Development[3] that we examined in Chapter 3. However, those relationships are easier spoken about than built. For myriad reasons, there can be real challenges in doing so. Some of this may be time-dependant, some may be because of a parent or carer's perception of ourselves as 'teachers', and their own personal experience of school.

Primary school staff are very good at building excellent relationships with parents, having strong and often daily communication with them, but for staff in seniors with 400 students a week, it can be a different ball game. Either way, we still have to prioritise, because there are plenty of students and families who will succeed with what we might think of as a 'standard' amount of contact – but others really do require more. We must be realistic. I know I said in the introduction that we can be heroes, but that doesn't mean we have magic wands secured in our backsides, ready to flourish at a moment's notice. Don't beat yourself up because you can't give an equal amount of attention to each parent in a school. Be **pragmatic**; not every family needs the same level of attention. This doesn't mean that you are not valuing each child just as much as all others, but you only have a certain amount of hours in a school year, so be realistic.

Building Trust

Just as we build trust with children, so we need to build trust with parents, and we need to show them that we are working with them because we have the best interests of their child at heart. That model of High Challenge and High Support that we looked at in Chapter 4, is just as important for parents as it is for the young people in our inclusive classroom. Working *with* parents, and not just doing things *for* them or *to* them, is the best way forwards.

Empathy is just as important here as it was back in Chapter 4 when we first examined using a PACE approach with young people. For families and parents, you will need to empathise with uncomfortable feelings such as:

Guilt, shame, fear, embarrassment, failure, judgement, intimidation, confusion.

I have referred to the work of Brené Brown a couple of times during this book. Her work is highly respected, with good reason, and she uses a definition of 'trust' that initially came from a gentleman named Charles Feltman.[4] This definition is the most impactful that I have come across, and when we hear it – and when we then apply it to a parent and their child – I think that it really brings home to us the position that we hold in schools. See if you agree:

> Trust: Choosing to risk making something you value vulnerable to another person's actions.

> Distrust: What is important to me is not safe with this person in this situation (or any situation).

> *(Feltman 2008)*

If we break this down and unpick it, parents are making their *child* – that which they hold most dear above all else in the world – **utterly vulnerable to our actions**. To the way we treat their child. To the way that others treat their child whilst we are in loco parentis. To the 6 hours or more a day that their child spends with us. To the way in which we speak to their child, think about their child, and educate their child. They are risking placing their child with us, based on the lone fact that we work in a school. Is it *any wonder* that some parents do not immediately trust us – just as some children do not? We must ensure that parents know that their child, in terms of education, socially, and emotionally (and in all manner of ways), is **safe with us**.

We must earn that trust and build those relationships. This is not a quick process. We have to listen to parents – really listen. Be mindful of what parents say. Show the parent that we are taking time and valuing them and their child. We need to build trust slowly, like popping pennies in a jar and building up a bank account of trust. Sometimes we might lose a pound or two after an incident, but we put in the right steps to then re-accumulate our loss with added interest on top. In essence, we need to show parents that we *care*. Meaningful contact, following through on things that we say we'll do, making contact for positives as well as negatives, and just giving a heartfelt smile at the end of the day, can make a huge difference.

Practical Ways to Build Trust

Don't wait for an issue: Teachers are adept at being able to spot a student who is beginning to cause concern. Rather than waiting for a problem, make contact with parents ASAP via small, positive messages, depositing pennies in the trust bank. This can be done easily by using whatever messaging platforms or methods your school makes available – such as messages that can be sent to entire classes or to individuals. It only takes minutes but can really make the difference to a parent's initial contact with staff.

Non-verbal empathy and Nonviolent Communication (NVC): Avoid trite phrases or 'at least … ' (remember our Empathy discussions in Chapter 4). Instead, when you speak to parents, use *non-verbal empathy* with your gestures and actions – if they are irate, remain calm and ensure your face and body language are displaying sympathy and understanding (as opposed to disbelief, irritation and so on). Use NVC with parents (Chapter 4) just as you do with the young people.

Tone of voice: Use a tone of voice that makes it clear that you empathise, that you're sure they're trying their hardest, and that you want the absolute best for their child. We all know what it's like when someone uses a tone that gets our back up - try your hardest to avoid doing so. Do not sound critical, you're on the same side, the one that benefits the student.

Don't over-promise, do what you say: If you say you're going to do something, do. And then let the parent know that you have, with the outcome. Be realistic with what you can do.

Follow-up contact: Make follow-up contact wherever you can - the more regular, the better. If you work in a primary school, then of course you can do this on the gate. Primary colleagues are wonderful at building that trust and connection, daily. In secondary schools, much of this can be via whatever messenger system you have, emails, or by using a go-between staff member who works with the family, such as a SEND teacher, or another appropriate staff member.

Declare your intention: Be open, say that you want to work together, be positive about the young person and what you hope to achieve, and that you want them to get the best outcomes. Use inclusive language like 'we', 'us', 'together we can', 'our'.

Learn how parents or carers like to be addressed: Is it Miss, Ms, Mr, Mrs? Are parents still together, is the student living with their birth parents or not? Ensure your pronunciation of names is correct.

Be curious about the young person and their parent: Use your PACE approach (Chapter 4). Ask questions, show that you're interested, do they have hobbies, or siblings, or a favourite place, and so on.

Thank parents and carers: Tell them you're grateful for their involvement, thank them for supporting you. If they've done so in a manner such as helping in class, or providing something for the class, then you can even thank them publicly in newsletters, if appropriate, and they do not mind the acknowledgement.

Keep a '5-4-Phoning' slot in your weekly diary: Have a 5-minute slot for phone calls each week. Choose one or two parents weekly to call with positive, celebratory news - it'll make their day, especially when unexpected.

Be thoughtful: Small gestures can make huge differences ...

- For example, emailing a link about an article re Speech and Language to a parent whose child would benefit, and saying that you thought of them when you saw it.
- Photocopying/scanning a piece of excellent work and sending/emailing it home because 'it's nice to hear the positives' and 'celebrate together'.
- Remembering that the family had a tricky appointment coming up or similar, and ringing just to check how it went - or use the school message system to ping them beforehand saying 'we are here to support' if needed.
- Add a 'How are you all?' to email replies if it's a parent you've not heard from in a while, just to show that you're thinking of family wellbeing.

The benefits to making the time - and taking the time - to build trust:

- Once parents trust the teachers, they trust the school. Barriers are broken down, bridges are built.

- Parents know that we'll do what we say we'll do.
- Parents will trust staff to have the best interests of their child at heart - and will therefore trust our professional opinions and our strategy suggestions.
- They will be more open to us, to trying things, to backing up staff - *to believing we have their child's **best interests** at heart, and not our own.*
- Parents will be more open to trying different suggestions at home and giving honest feedback to teachers about what did or didn't work.
- Parents will be better placed to understand the teachers' viewpoints because of good, honest, and open conversations.
- If parents feel listened to, appreciated, empathised with, and valued (as opposed to judged, blamed, ashamed), then we get their backing - and the children benefit.

 Out of the Mouths of Parents

When my son first started in Year R, I found it incredibly hard to believe that he'd be cared for in a class of 30, or that anyone would really get to know him. He had unidentified needs at that point, and I was surprised when his teacher contacted me not long after he started and told me what she'd noticed. They quickly put some supportive strategies in place and I was always made to feel welcome – as opposed to being like a pain in the backside – if I felt the need to speak with her at the start or end of a day. If she didn't have time, she'd let me know and say she'd call me – and she always did, so I totally trusted her. It was a great start to school for him and me!

My son has SEND and I have regular contact from a SEND teacher at his school. This means that I am informed but it also means that I feel like I'm included in everything. I don't worry as much anymore because I've now worked with the SEND teacher for over a year and we've developed a level of trust. The school appreciate how stressful it is for me, so I get some emotional support from them too, and that's really helpful because I know they understand both my son and me.

When my daughter first started secondary school, I couldn't believe how little I knew about her day, her teachers, the building, how she was doing – it's a different world to primary and it takes a lot to get used to. You go from daily contact to a yearly Parents' Evening, and a weekly newsletter! You get used to it but it's a lot to adjust to at first.

My son is in Year 8. There were problems with his support and the delivery of his EHCP in his primary school, which was upsetting for me. However, teachers in his secondary school have been invaluable and very important to me and my son. The SENDCO there took over his care requirements, planning of his support and became my main contact with the school, but his class teachers also make an effort to send me positive messages. The school ensured that my son has access to everything his EHCP stipulates and the SENDCO and his tutor have been reassuring to me as a SEND parent, answering questions and dealing with queries efficiently and effectively. The staff are personable, friendly, empathic, understanding, kind and reassuring. They have renewed my faith in school with regards to my son's needs. Their approach is always focused on the needs of my child. My son is thriving in seniors in no small part to their knowledge and care.

I've had a range of experiences throughout primary school for my son and the most positive ones have always come about because of strong communication from teachers who actually care. This hasn't depended on their level of experience or age, it's purely been down to the person that they are and their own attitudes. At the end of the day, if you can see that somebody cares, then you're automatically on the same side aren't you? Which is a good starting place.

Whenever there's been an issue at school, my son's teacher always contacts me and always starts the conversation by telling me 'not to worry'. It's a small thing I know, but when I see the school number on my phone, the first thing I do is worry, so this sets me at ease and I'm less defensive or fearful to start the conversation than I might otherwise be.

Notes

1 National Award for Special Educational Needs Co-ordination.
2 https://d2tic4wvo1iusb.cloudfront.net/eef-guidance-reports/teaching-assistants/TA
 _Recommendations_Summary.pdf?v=1685097377
3 https://news.harvard.edu/gazette/story/2017/04/over-nearly-80-years-harvard-study
 -has-been-showing-how-to-live-a-healthy-and-happy-life/
4 https://brenebrown.com/art/a-good-word-charles-feltman-on-trust-and-distrust/

References

Education Endowment Foundation. (2018). *Making the Best Use of Teaching Assistants*. Available at: https://d2tic4wvo1iusb.cloudfront.net/eef-guidance-reports/teaching-assistants/TA_Guidance _Report_MakingBestUseOfTeachingAssistants-Printable_2021-11-02-162019_wsqd.pdf?v =1685097377

Education Endowment Foundation. (2020, updated 2021). *SEND in Mainstream Schools: A Guidance Report.* Available at: https://educationendowmentfoundation.org.uk/education-evidence/guidance-reports/send

Feltman, C. (2008). *The Thin Book of Trust: An Essential Primer for Building Trust at Work.* Thin Book Publishing Company.

A Final Word

And so, we have reached the end of our relational journey together here in terms of this book - but hopefully it's only the beginning of yours in school. And remember, each *day* is a new beginning in school. Each lesson, even.

It is never easy and, if it were, we wouldn't enjoy it as much as we do.

Use this book to dip into and dip out of. Use it to inspire you, encourage you, and help you to build your toolkit of approaches and adaptations. Use it to help you inspire others, and to make those fabled and positive differences that we all come into teaching to achieve. As my dear dad, Pete Lush, once said, *it matters all the time*. And so do you.

Everything begins with teaching. Each career in the world began with somebody being taught something, somewhere. The future begins with teaching. The future begins with supporting the young minds in our inclusive classrooms. The future begins with *you*.

Instagram: @veritylush

DOI: 10.4324/b23417-9

APPENDIX

How and where each chapter corresponds with the Education Endowment Foundation (EEF)'s Guidance Report for SEND in Mainstream Schools (2020) (See Chapter 5)

5 EEF Recommendations SEND in Mainstream Schools Guidance Report, p. 8–9	Create a positive and supportive environment for all pupils, without exception	Build an ongoing, holistic understanding of your pupils and their needs	Ensure all pupils have access to high-quality teaching	Complement high-quality teaching with carefully selected small-group and one-to-one interventions	Work effectively with teaching assistants
	Essentially, this never stops – it's part of our relational foundation. **Chapter 1** What does 'inclusion' mean? The Early Career Framework (ECF). Differences between differentiation and adaptive teaching. Your own wellbeing. **Chapter 2** How to talk about SEND. Areas of Need. Neurodiversity.	**Essentially, this never stops – it's part of our relational foundation.** **Chapter 1** Working with one another, doing things with and not to. Adapting for yourself. **Chapter 2** Our base knowledge of SEND & the Four Broad Areas of Need. Your SENDCO. The SEND Code of Practice.	**Chapter 1** Excellent teaching for pupils with SEND is excellent teaching for all. The ECF around adaptive teaching as opposed to differentiating and pigeonholing students into learning styles or abilities. **Chapter 2** 'High-Quality Teaching' and the SEND Code of Practice. Knowledge of the Four Broad Areas of Need, neurodiversity, and being needs-led (not waiting for diagnoses).	**Chapter 1, 2, 3** Identification of children who require this, working with year group leads, subject leads, and the SENDCO – the latter will usually organise and arrange implementation. If you are likely to be delivering these, then again your SENDCO will make clear what that targeted intervention will look like and incorporate. Some students with support plans (such as legally binding ones, EHCPs and so forth) will have interventions written into these. It's the responsibility of the SENDCO to ensure they are implemented.	**Chapter 2** Legally binding support and support staff. **Chapter 7** Being inclusive of the other adults in the room. Never 'ignoring' the child because they have adult support – or speaking to the supporting adult and not the child. Testimonies from support staff regarding what they believe in their experiences leads to best outcomes for the children. Relational approaches with *all* stakeholders. Trust and families, and building relationships and trust with parents and carers.

5 EEF Recommendations SEND in Mainstream Schools Guidance Report, p. 8-9	Create a positive and supportive environment for all pupils, without exception	Build an ongoing, holistic understanding of your pupils and their needs	Ensure all pupils have access to high-quality teaching	Complement high-quality teaching with carefully selected small-group and one-to-one interventions	Work effectively with teaching assistants
	Chapter 3 Relational approaches: the what and the why. Always maintaining unconditional positive regard. Building connections. Trust and Maslow's Hierarchy of Needs. Social, Emotional and Mental Health (SEMH) and exclusion. Adverse Childhood Experiences (ACEs) and readily available trusted adults. Trauma Informed Approaches. **Chapter 4** High challenge, high support. Working with, not doing to.	Looking for the cause to support the effect. Being Needs-Led. Legally binding documents of support – EHCPs. **Chapter 3** Trust and Maslow's Hierarchy of Needs. Unconditional positive regard. Relationships outside of school (including lockdowns and screentime as opposed to in-person social connection). ACEs and Readily available trusted adults. Trauma Informed Approaches. Kindness.	**Chapter 3** What 'teaching' is in the 21st century. Adapting our approaches using relational pedagogies as part and parcel of High-Quality Teaching. SEMH. High expectations for all students Supporting students to become future-ready. **Chapter 5** The EEF's 5 strategies. Rosenshine's Principles of Instruction. Practical Strategies for adapting our teaching. Adapting our teaching using Play and PACE and experiential learning.	Your adaptive and high quality teaching in-class may negate the need for intervention, but if not, liaise with your SENDCO and/or learning support. Cause and Effect Model throughout the book – identification of needs, meeting those, using your SENDCO to support you. **Chapter 6** What it looks like in practice and how to use your knowledge to adapt your teaching.	

5 EEF Recommendations SEND in Mainstream Schools Guidance Report, p. 8–9	Create a positive and supportive environment for all pupils, without exception	Build an ongoing, holistic understanding of your pupils and their needs	Ensure all pupils have access to high-quality teaching	Complement high-quality teaching with carefully selected small-group and one-to-one interventions	Work effectively with teaching assistants
	Behaviour and meaningful consequences.	**Chapter 4** Building trust. Relational pedagogies. Relationships and family dynamics. The science of neglect. **Chapter 5** The model for our inclusive classroom. Knowledge and skills. The EEF guidance around High-Quality Teaching. Rosenshine's Principles of Instruction. Practical Strategies for adapting our teaching. Adapting our teaching using Play and PACE, and experiential learning.	**Chapter 6** Bringing it all together. What it looks like in practice. Nonviolent communication. Name It to Tame It. How we speak with children. Our non-verbal cues and body language. Emotional Intelligence. Six Principles of Nurture. Relational/Restorative Practice. PACE. The science of neglect. **Chapter 5** Using the EEF guidance around High-Quality Teaching. Using Rosenshine's Principles.		

5 EEF Recommendations SEND in Mainstream Schools Guidance Report, p. 8-9	Create a positive and supportive environment for all pupils, without exception	Build an ongoing, holistic understanding of your pupils and their needs	Ensure all pupils have access to high-quality teaching	Complement high-quality teaching with carefully selected small-group and one-to-one interventions	Work effectively with teaching assistants
		Chapter 6 Our knowledge and understanding of non-legally binding documents for SEND and required support (Pupil Passports and so forth) and how to now use these. **Chapter 7** Relationships with parents. How other adults in the classroom help us to get to know the children.	Practical strategies for using the P from PACE (playfulness) to adapt our teaching and our resources, including Experiential Learning. **Chapter 6** Bringing it all together. What it looks like in practice. Making the most of documents of support. **Chapter 7** Making the best and most effective use of adults in the classroom. Building relationships with parents and carers.		

Reference

Education Endowment Foundation. (2020, updated 2021). *SEND in Mainstream Schools: A Guidance Report*. Available at: https://educationendowmentfoundation.org.uk/education-evidence/guidance-reports/send

INDEX

Page numbers in *italics* denote figures.

Printed in the United States
by Baker & Taylor Publisher Services

Printed in the United States
by Baker & Taylor Publisher Services